BEC

HIGHER
Practice Tests

Four tests for the Cambridge Business English Certificate

MARK HARRISON • ROSALIE KERR
Series editors:
Mark Harrison and Rosalie Kerr

ADVANCED

with answers

OXFORD
UNIVERSITY PRESS

OXFORD
UNIVERSITY PRESS

Great Clarendon Street, Oxford OX2 6DP

Oxford University Press is a department of the University of Oxford.
It furthers the University's objective of excellence in research,
scholarship, and education by publishing worldwide in

Oxford   New York

Athens   Auckland   Bangkok   Bogotá   Buenos Aires
Cape Town   Chennai   Dar es Salaam   Delhi   Florence   Hong Kong
Istanbul   Karachi   Kolkata   Kuala Lumpur   Madrid   Melbourne
Mexico City   Mumbai   Nairobi   Paris   São Paulo   Shanghai   Singapore
Taipei   Tokyo   Toronto   Warsaw

with associated companies in   Berlin   Ibadan

Oxford and Oxford English are registered trade marks of
Oxford University Press in the UK and in certain other countries

© Oxford University Press 2002

The moral rights of the author have been asserted

Database right Oxford University Press (maker)

First published 2002

All rights reserved. No part of this publication may be reproduced,
stored in a retrieval system, or transmitted, in any form or by any
means, without the prior permission in writing of Oxford University
Press, or as expressly permitted by law, or under terms agreed
with the appropriate reprographics rights organization. Enquiries
concerning reproduction outside the scope of the above should be
sent to the ELT Rights Department, Oxford University Press,
at the address above

You must not circulate this book in any other binding or cover
and you must impose this same condition on any acquirer

Photocopying

The Publisher grants permission for the photocopying of those
pages marked 'photocopiable' according to the following conditions.
Individual purchasers may make copies for their own use or for use
by classes that they teach. School purchasers may make copies for
use by staff and students, but this permission does not extend to
additional schools or branches

Under no circumstances may any part of this book be photocopied
for resale

ISBN 0 19 453187 2

Printed in Hong Kong

Acknowledgements

The authors and publisher are grateful to those who have given
permission to reproduce the following extracts and adaptations of
copyright material:

p7 Advertisements for vacancies with Sales Associates. Reproduced
by permission of Sales Associates Limited.

Reproduced by permission of Haymarket Business Publications Ltd:
p8 'Don't let wafflers waste your time' by Winston Fletcher,
Management Today November 1998.
p30 'The Dominant e-mail' by Jane Bird, *Management Today*,
November 1998.
p43 'Readings and rankings' book reviews (B & C), *Management
Today*, July 1998.
p61 'Never put off until tomorrow...' by Winston Fletcher,
Management Today, January 1999.
p62 'The one-to-one gap' by Alan Mitchell, *Management Today*, July
1998.

Reproduced by permission of Telegraph Group Limited:
p12 'Get motivated in staff encouragement' by Adrian Furnham, *The
Daily Telegraph*, 22 October 1998.
p28 'Bullying no substitute for leadership' by Hugh Thompson, *The
Sunday Telegraph*, 14 February 1999.
p33 'Is there an editor in the house?' by Craig Seton, *The Daily
Telegraph*, 17 March 1999.
p46 'Focus groups fail to reach pin-sharp results' by Adrian Furnham,
The Sunday Telegraph, 4 October 1998.
p48 'Firms lose their fear of fifty and see older workers as just the job'
by David White, *The Daily Telegraph*, 20 May 1999.
p50 'Banging on the drum for the one-man band' by Michael Becket,
The Daily Telegraph, 7 October 1996.
p64 'Sing from the same song sheet to achieve your perfect harmony'
by Hugh Thompson, *The Daily Telegraph*, 26 November 1998.

p10 Extracts from 'Working with Emotional Intelligence' by Daniel
Goleman. Reproduced by permission of Daniel Goleman and
Bloomsbury Publishing Plc.
p14 'Brands that came out of the vending closet' © Amanda Roberts /
Times Newspapers Limited, 20 March 1997. Reproduced by
permission.
p15 Extracts from 'Getting Jobs in Advertising' by Jenny Timber
published by Cassell & Co.
p26 'Rally to the company colours and kick for the common goal' by
Phillip Schofield, *The Sunday Telegraph*, 29 March 1998. Reproduced
by permission of Phillip Schofield.
p43 Management of Diversity book reviews (A & D) taken from
Professional Manager, July 1998. Reproduced by permission of The
Institute of Management.
p44 'Secretarial: It doesn't have to hurt', Kate Hilpern, *The
Independent*, 18 November 1998, Reproduced by permission of
Independent Newspapers (UK) Limited.
p66 'Focus on the future of work' by Professor Peter Nolan,
Professional Manager, July 1998. Published by The Institute of
Management with acknowledgement to the Economic and Social
Research Council, who funded the research upon which the article was
based. Reproduced by permission of The Institute of Management.
p69 'Tailor-made to meet your needs' by Robert Craven, *The Daily
Telegraph*, 3 September 1998. Reproduced by permission of Robert
Craven.
p100 'My big break – Upwards with the gadgets from Hull' by
Caroline Rees, *The Guardian*, 23 October 1999. Reproduced by
permission of Caroline Rees.
pp102–3 'Getting a grip on absence' by Helen Gregson, *Spectrum*
Spring 1999. Reproduced by permission of Watson Wyatt Worldwide.

Although every effort has been made to trace and contact copyright
holders before publication, this has not been possible in some cases.
We apologize for any apparent infringement of copyright and if
notified, the publisher will be pleased to rectify any errors or
omissions at the earliest opportunity.

The authors and publisher are grateful to the University of Cambridge
Local Examinations Syndicate for permission to reproduce the sample
answer sheets on pp78–80, the Writing marking information on p81,
and the Speaking Criteria on p110.

The authors and publisher would also like to thank the following
students and schools for providing sample student answers on
pp82–96: Li Xiu Zhen from the East Finchley School of English; Ursula
Reiling, Annette Kaelin, Carlo Favero, Mirjam Suter, Yannick Lesage
from KV Business School, Zurich.

Contents

Introduction — 4

TEST 1
Reading — 6
Writing — 16
Listening — 18
Speaking — 22

TEST 2
Reading — 24
Writing — 34
Listening — 36
Speaking — 40

TEST 3
Reading — 42
Writing — 52
Listening — 54
Speaking — 58

TEST 4
Reading — 60
Writing — 70
Listening — 72
Speaking — 76

Answer Sheets — 78

Writing General Mark Scheme — 81

Key — 82

Tapescripts — 98

Speaking Assessment Criteria — 110

Introduction

The **Business English Certificates (BEC)** are examinations aimed primarily at learners who wish to obtain a business-related English language qualification. There are three exams: Preliminary (Lower Intermediate), Vantage (Upper Intermediate) and Higher (Advanced). Each level tests the four language skills: Reading, Writing, Listening and Speaking.

This book contains **four** complete practice tests for the **BEC Higher** exam.

READING   1 hour

PART	TEXT	QUESTION TYPE	NO. OF QUS. / MARKS
1	5 separate short texts OR 5 short extracts from a single text (about 450 words in total)	8 sentences which have to be matched to texts or extracts.	8
2	1 text with 6 gaps (about 450 – 500 words)	Choose which sentence fills each gap from a choice of 7.	6
3	1 longer text (about 500 – 600 words)	6 multiple-choice questions, each with 4 options, testing comprehension of details, opinions, etc.	6
4	1 text with 10 gaps (about 250 words)	10 multiple-choice questions mostly testing vocabulary. Choose from 4 options the word or phrase that fills each gap.	10
5	1 text with 10 gaps (about 250 words)	Fill each gap with one word. This part mostly tests grammar.	10
6	1 text with some errors (about 150 – 200 words)	Identify the errors (extra words which should not be there) and the correct lines.	12
			TOTAL = 52

WRITING   1 hour 10 minutes

PART	TASK	LENGTH
1	Write a short report based on one or more graphics (charts, graphs, etc). Answers involve describing, comparing and interpreting the information presented.	120 – 140 words
2	Write **one** of the following: **report, proposal**, OR **piece of correspondence**. Answers are based on the context and instructions for content given in the question.	200 – 250 words

LISTENING   about 40 minutes

PART	WHAT YOU HEAR	QUESTION TYPE	NO. OF QUS / MARKS
1	1 monologue (about 600 words)	Filling 12 gaps with words, numbers or short phrases providing information given in the monologue.	12
2	5 short monologues relating to a single theme or topic (about 130 words each)	**Two** tasks, each involving choosing which of 8 options matches what each of the speakers says (5 questions per task).	10
3	1 longer conversation, interview or discussion, involving two or more speakers (about 600 – 700 words)	8 multiple-choice questions, each with 3 options, testing comprehension of details, opinions, etc. given by the speakers.	8
			TOTAL = 30

SPEAKING   about 16 minutes (usually two candidates and two examiners)

PART	ACTIVITY	LENGTH
1	Conversation between candidate and examiner, during which the candidate gives personal information and opinions.	about 3 mins
2	Each candidate gives a one-minute talk or presentation on a business theme, based on different prompts which they are given. Each candidate chooses from three prompts the one they are going to talk about. Candidates are asked to respond to each other's talk.	about 6 mins
3	Conversation / discussion between the two candidates based on a prompt given to both of them. The prompt contains a business context and two discussion points. The conversation / discussion then continues with the examiner taking part.	about 7 mins

BEC is held six times per year (in March, May, June, July, November and December) at centres worldwide. Details of the entry procedure, current fees and further information about this and other Cambridge examinations can be obtained from the Local Secretary for UCLES examinations in your area or from:

EFL Information
University of Cambridge
  Local Examinations Syndicate
1 Hills Road
Cambridge
CB1 2EU
United Kingdom

Tel: +44 1223 553355
Fax: +44 1223 460278
www.cambridge-efl.org.uk
e-mail: efl@ucles.org.uk

Test One Reading

TEST ONE
READING
(1 hour)

Part 1
Questions 1–8

- Look at the statements below and at the five advertisements for jobs connected with sales on the opposite page.
- Which advert (**A, B, C, D** or **E**) does each statement **1–8** refer to?
- For each statement **1–8**, mark **one** letter (**A, B, C, D** or **E**) on your Answer Sheet.
- You will need to use some of these letters more than once.

Example:
    0   This post is in a field in which most companies are similar to each other.

1   This post is with a company that has taken over other companies.

2   The successful candidate for this post may be promoted quickly.

3   This post involves working out precisely what customers wish to achieve.

4   The successful candidate for this post will be someone whose method of selling is not aggressive.

5   This post involves preventing a certain limit from being exceeded.

6   This post is with a company that mentions having a general policy regarding its treatment of its employees.

7   This post is with a company whose approach is seen as being original.

8   This post requires someone who can show that they have been successful in a particular kind of work.

6

A

Sponsorship Sales Manager

International Conferences

This company provides busy professionals with comprehensive networking opportunities, designed to address the latest critical developments and industry innovations that affect business organisations throughout the world. Your role will be to establish a clear strategy to fully exploit conference sponsorship opportunities, optimise revenues and manage sponsor relations. As well as a proven track record of selling high value business-to-business products, you must demonstrate good interpersonal and presentation skills, initiative and a determination to succeed. Prove yourself, and your progress within this dynamic organisation will be swift.

B

Trainee Consultant Executive

Sales Recruitment

In an increasingly sophisticated recruitment industry, it is hard to differentiate yourself. As the biggest in finance recruitment, this company has been able to do just that. As a result, our clients are some of the most prestigious investment banks and companies in the world. As a trainee consultant, you will be instrumental in identifying every single potential candidate within a given market for any particular assignment. You must possess excellent verbal communication skills, a consultative sales style and enjoy working under pressure in a high-energy environment.

C

Display Sales Executive

Publishing House

Through organic growth and shrewd acquisition, this company has grown rapidly to become one of the major business press publishing houses in the UK. An opportunity now exists for a dynamic and motivated sales person to develop and fully exploit the potential of four leading titles. The role involves selling to a client base of car manufacturers and associated companies. As the range of products expands, there is also an opportunity to become involved with exhibitions, conferences and new media in an environment where you can make an immediate impact.

D

Sales Executive

Training Consultancy

In the 20 years since this company was founded, it has become one of the country's most respected and influential consultancies of its kind, through providing individually tailored and innovative consultancy and training services. A need has arisen for an experienced telesales person to build on the success to date and develop new opportunities. Determined and self-motivated, you will have exemplary interpersonal skills and enjoy building relationships with clients in order to define their needs and objectives. The working environment is busy, team-spirited and focused on providing a level of customer care that is second to none.

E

Experienced Sales Manager

Conference Company

This young, dynamic conference company in the financial services sector is looking for a results and revenue driven motivator. You should have a high level of commercial acumen and possess initiative, vision and ambition. Key responsibilities of this post include participation in the recruitment of the sales team and participation in the drawing up of a departmental budget and ensuring that it is adhered to. The post carries an attractive remuneration package, including a generous basic salary and unlimited commission, plus management opportunities for the right person – reflecting the company's ethos of rewarding results and achievement.

Part 2

Questions 9–14

- Read this text taken from an article about time management.
- Choose the best sentence from the opposite page to fill each of the gaps.
- For each gap **9–14**, mark **one** letter (**A–H**) on your Answer Sheet.
- Do not mark any letter more than once.
- There is an example at the beginning (**0**).

TIME MANAGEMENT FOR MANAGERS

Most managers' days are disorderly and disorganised, which means there is vast room for improvement. **(0)** ..*H*.. So how can you manage your time more efficiently?

The first and most crucial step is to keep a time log for a few weeks. Nobody enjoys this. Just keeping the time log itself at first seems to absorb an inordinate amount of time. Yet, within a couple of days, it will seem to take no time at all. You may even feel a compulsion to record the timekeeping itself. It can become addictive, but it is rarely worth keeping a log permanently. **(9)**......

A time log is just a diary in which the time you have spent is divided up, usually under these headings: meetings (in groups); meetings (one-to-one); writing letters; writing documents; talking on the telephone; handling interruptions; dealing with crises; and thinking/planning. **(10)**...... It is vital to complete each day's log that evening or, at the latest, next morning. Memories are too fallible to let things slide. And don't cheat. If you've spent time gossiping or reading a magazine, log it. **(11)**......

After a few weeks, the ways in which you have been spending your time will become, often depressingly, apparent. **(12)**...... This is likely to be the opposite of how you spend your time now!

Almost certainly, you will find that interruptions are the most pernicious time-wasters, and dealing with them is a vital part of time management. In my view, open-plan offices and hot-desking exacerbate the problem. Some unplanned visitations are necessary, some unnecessary and some simply run too long. Here are some ways to deal with them.

Set time limits. As soon as the visitor arrives, simply say: 'Do you mind if we wrap this up in eight or nine minutes, as I've an awful lot on?' Using a specific, slightly quirky time availability helps get the message across. Refer the visitor elsewhere. When you learn the reason for the visit, say politely but firmly: 'X could deal with this better than **(13)**...... Get it in writing. As soon as the visitor has started, interrupt and say: 'I'm sorry, I hadn't realised how important this is. Could you send me a memo or e-mail?' Visit the visitor. If they are people who talk a lot without getting to the point, don't let them get started but offer to go to them later. **(14)**...... Above all, the best way to deal with visitors is to block out a period every couple of days and ask drop-ins whose business is not urgent to come back then. It works a treat.

Example:

- **A** Depending on your job, you might add travel, dealing with customers and any other important facet of your job.

- **B** This avoids spending time discussing issues that are not your business and that you are not empowered to resolve.

- **C** It is much easier for you to leave your place than to get someone else to leave it.

- **D** At least you will have taken care of the most important things, without getting distracted by items of lesser importance.

- **E** The insights into the way you spend your working day can be gleaned quite quickly.

- **F** Only when you know the truth can you decide whether or not to change your habits.

- **G** From then on, you will be able to start ensuring that you devote more time to tasks of great importance and less to those that hardly matter.

- **H** Even quite small reforms can yield worthwhile dividends.

Part 3
Questions 15-20

- Read the following extract from a book about behaviour at work and the questions on the opposite page.
- For each question **15-20**, mark **one** letter (**A**, **B**, **C** or **D**) on your Answer Sheet for the answer you choose.

The rules for work are changing. We're being judged by a new yardstick: not just by how smart we are, or by our training and expertise, but also by how well we handle each other. This yardstick is increasingly applied in choosing who will be hired and who will not, who will be let go and who retained, who passed over and who promoted. The new rules predict who is most likely to become a star performer and who is most prone to derailing. And, no matter what field we work in currently, they measure the traits that are crucial to our marketability for future jobs. They take for granted having enough intellectual ability and technical know-how to do our jobs and focus instead on personal qualities such as initiative and empathy, adaptability and persuasiveness.

Talked about loosely for decades under a variety of names, from 'character' and 'personality' to 'soft skills' and 'competence', there is at last a more precise understanding of these human talents, and a new name for them: 'emotional intelligence'. Emotional intelligence is generally defined as the ability to monitor and regulate one's own and others' feelings, and to use feelings to guide thought and action. Emotional intelligence in work life comprises five basic elements: self-awareness, self-regulation, motivation, empathy and adeptness in relationships. It does not mean merely 'being nice'. At strategic moments it may demand not 'being nice', but rather, for example, bluntly confronting someone with the uncomfortable truth. Nor does emotional intelligence mean giving free rein to feelings – 'letting it all hang out'. Rather, it means managing feelings so that they are expressed appropriately and effectively, enabling people to work together smoothly toward their common goal.

More and more companies are seeing that encouraging emotional intelligence skills is a vital component of any organisation's management philosophy. And the more complex the job, the more emotional intelligence matters – if only because a deficiency in these abilities can hinder the use of whatever technical expertise or intellect a person may have. To be sure, many people have risen to the top despite flaws in emotional intelligence, but as work becomes more complex and collaborative, companies where people work together best have a competitive edge. In the new workplace, with its emphasis on flexibility, teams, and a strong customer orientation, this crucial set of emotional competencies is becoming increasingly essential for excellence in every job and in every part of the world.

The good news is that emotional intelligence can be learnt. Studies that have tracked people's level of emotional intelligence through the years show that people get better and better in these capabilities as they grow more adept at handling their own emotions and impulses, at motivating themselves, and at honing their empathy and social adroitness. There is an old-fashioned word for this: maturity. And although emotional intelligence is no magic bullet, no guarantee of more market share or a healthier bottom line, if the human ingredient is ignored, then nothing else works as well as it might.

However, simply being high in emotional intelligence does not guarantee a person will have learned the practical emotional skills that matter for work. For example, a person may be highly sensitive to others' feelings, and yet not have learned the skills based on empathy that translate into superior customer service, top-flight coaching, or the ability to bring together a diverse work team.

15 What changes with regard to work does the writer mention in the first paragraph?

　　A　Intellectual and technical ability are no longer valued as highly as they were.
　　B　Employees now have higher expectations of each other.
　　C　The potential of employees is now assessed by new criteria.
　　D　Some of the inaccurate judgements that used to be made are no longer made.

16 The writer says that the term 'emotional intelligence'

　　A　is unlikely to remain in fashion for long.
　　B　is very difficult to define.
　　C　has previously been misunderstood.
　　D　has replaced less suitable terms.

17 According to the writer, emotional intelligence does not involve

　　A　expressing your emotions all the time.
　　B　acting kindly towards others most of the time.
　　C　focusing on a single aim.
　　D　showing that you are angry with someone.

18 Why, according to the writer, is emotional intelligence seen as vital?

　　A　Emphasis on it prevents the wrong people from being given senior positions.
　　B　It enables people to meet the challenges set by changes in the nature of work.
　　C　Lack of it makes the recruitment of good employees difficult.
　　D　It can compensate for a lack of technical or intellectual ability.

19 What does the writer say about emotional intelligence in the fourth paragraph?

　　A　It is often seen as the cure for any problem a company faces.
　　B　It develops naturally in people.
　　C　Some people possess it more than others.
　　D　Understanding of it has increased over a period of time.

20 The writer concludes in the final paragraph that emotional intelligence

　　A　sometimes causes people to make unwise decisions at work.
　　B　is not particularly useful in certain areas of work.
　　C　will soon be valued even more highly than it is now.
　　D　may not enable someone to be good at their job.

Part 4

Questions 21–30

- Read the article below about employees who lack motivation.
- Choose the correct word to fill each gap from **A**, **B**, **C** or **D** on the opposite page.
- For each question **21–30**, mark **one** letter (**A**, **B**, **C** or **D**) on your Answer Sheet.
- There is an example at the beginning (**0**).

NO JOB SATISFACTION

Managers, company owners and supervisors have always been (0)..B.. and bewildered by the employee with little or no work motivation. We have all seen the employee who has little or no commitment and just goes through the (21)...... . Nothing seems to fire them up, making firing them a real option. They shrewdly avoid doing anything that (22)...... dismissal and seem content to (23)...... their heads down, doing the minimum and volunteering nothing.

In the modern economy, many organisations have taught individuals that they work for themselves, because organisations will not or cannot (24)...... jobs five, even two years from now. Thus, anybody who is not considering moving elsewhere is a fool. Company loyalty really only means not looking for your next job on the company's (25)...... . Some feel it is foolish to be loyal to a company that is not loyal to them. The relationship between employers and employees is increasingly (26)...... on both sides. Hence, many employees feel about their organisation: 'If you use me, I'll use you.'

So what have the management gurus produced in the way of new techniques for motivation? The answer, it seems, is not a lot. Ideas about motivation get repackaged and renamed but (27)...... remain the same as ever. The fact that they know some of the key factors in motivation has not prevented many managers from (28)...... them. This is because few managers are trained in the (29)...... and have themselves never been well managed, and so one gets the (30)...... of incompetence. That explains why people seem to have heard about, but not seen, successful motivational management in practice.

Example:

	A irritable	B frustrated	C heated	D furious

0 | A ☐ B ■ C ☐ D ☐

21	A gestures	B pretences	C motions	D indications
22	A warrants	B entitles	C sanctions	D empowers
23	A set	B hold	C turn	D keep
24	A reassure	B undertake	C commit	D guarantee
25	A time	B hours	C period	D days
26	A advantageous	B capitalised	C exploitative	D imposing
27	A radically	B fundamentally	C vitally	D primarily
28	A overseeing	B ignoring	C slipping	D passing
29	A aptitude	B gift	C art	D mastery
30	A perpetuation	B endurance	C perseverance	D duration

Part 5
Questions 31–40

- Read the article below about machines that sell drinks.
- For each question **31–40**, write **one** word in CAPITAL LETTERS on your Answer Sheet.

Example: `0 A R E`

THE GROWTH OF BIG NAMES ON DRINKS MACHINES

Brands sell products. Retailers and brand manufacturers worldwide (0)......... well aware of the power of the brand name. They know that (31)....... advertising where a big brand is on offer, they can significantly increase sales. Vending – selling products such as food and drink in machines – is in many ways an extension of the retail industry, but it was slow to wake up to the potential of big brands. However, once it (32)....... so, progress was rapid.

Just a few years ago, most machines (33)....... feature some sort of dull design on a boring brown, grey or white cabinet machine. Today, machines are fully branded to promote the product on sale and a vending machine (34)....... become essentially one huge advertising panel. The soft drinks manufacturers were the first (35)....... recognise the potential of branding machines and eventually the rest of the industry started to follow suit.

Development of branded vending in sectors other (36)....... canned soft drinks was slow, largely due to the reluctance of brand owners to put their names on machines over (37)....... they had no control and which may be serving a poor product. It is an indication of how quality has improved in the market and how perception of vending has changed (38)....... brand owners are now quite happy to put their names to, and promote, the product dispensed. Branding does work for vending. It gains (39)....... confidence of the consumer that the product which will be dispensed is one which they recognise and with which they associate (40)....... certain quality. This builds loyalty with the consumer and increases sales.

Part 6

Questions 41–52

- Read the text below about marketing.
- In most of the lines **41–52**, there is one extra word. It is either grammatically incorrect or does not fit in with the sense of the text. Some lines, however, are correct.
- If a line is correct, write **CORRECT** on your Answer Sheet.
- If there is an extra word in the line, write **the extra word** in CAPITAL LETTERS on your Answer Sheet.
- The exercise begins with two examples (**0**) and (**00**).

Examples: | 0 | S | O | M | E | | | |

| 00 | C | O | R | R | E | C | T |

WHAT IS MARKETING?

0 People interested in advertising as a career are often also some interested in

00 marketing, and quite rightly so, as the two are closely linked. When asked what

41 marketing is, the reply is often that it is quite to do with selling, which is true.

42 However, marketing is more than selling: it's deciding what will likely sell and to

43 whom, getting it designed, manufactured, priced and too packaged, promoting and

44 advertising it, and *then* selling it. Marketing is, therefore, a wider concept than

45 advertising or selling. This is something that has to be fully understood by the staff

46 of an advertising agency, who so may need to argue with the marketing department

47 of a client that its marketing policy is being at fault and that unless the name, price

48 or distribution of the product is changed, the advertising campaign will sure be

49 useless. Marketing is a very important activity to any kind business venture. To

50 make something, no matter how far technologically marvellous, and then hope that

51 there are people out there who will buy it, is a risky business. While it's more

52 sensible to find out if there is a market for a proposed product or what gaps there

   are in an existing market. That's where marketing comes in.

WRITING

(1 hour 10 minutes)

Part 1

Question 1

- The pie charts below show the composition of the workforce of a manufacturing company called AVC by age group for the years 1980 and 2000.
- Using the information in the charts, write a short **report** describing the changes which took place between 1980 and 2000.
- Write **120–140** words on the Answer Paper.

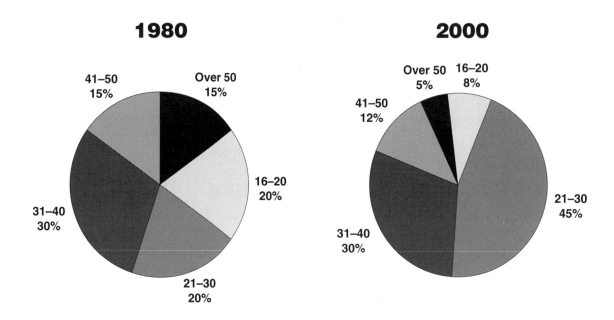

Part 2

Answer **ONE** of the questions 2, 3 or 4 below.

Question 2

- For the last year, the company you work for has been outsourcing staff training programmes in IT skills to a firm of consultants. It is now time to decide whether to renew the contract. There have been some problems, and the Directors have asked you to write a report before this decision is made.
- Write the **report**, outlining the successes and failures of the contract, and referring to the following points:
    - the suitability and relevance of the courses to the company's needs
    - the quality of the training personnel and materials
    - whether the contract was cost effective
    - whether you recommend renewing the contract.
- Write **200–250** words on the Answer Paper.

Question 3

- All new permanent employees with your company spend their first day in an introductory programme. This takes the form of talks to small groups on the company history and structure, health and safety rules, etc. The Head of Human Resources has now decided to replace some of this programme with a video, and has asked you to write a proposal for this.
- Write the **proposal**, explaining the advantages of having a video, and including the following points:
    - which parts of the existing programme should be replaced by the video, which should remain as they are, and why
    - which internal staff will be involved in making the video and what external consultants will be needed
    - an estimate of how long it will take to complete this project.
- Write **200–250** words on the Answer Paper.

Question 4

- Your company is developing a new product and has reached a stage where it would like to get some public reactions to the product. You have decided to draft a letter which will be sent to appropriate members of the public, explaining your plans for trialling the product, and asking them to take part in the trials.
- Write the **letter**, giving details of the following points:
    - what the product is and why you are planning to trial it
    - what the procedure for trialling will involve
    - what people who wish to take part in the trialling should do
    - what reward will be offered to those who decide to take part.
- Write **200–250** words on the Answer Paper.

Test One   Listening

LISTENING
(about 40 minutes)

Part 1

Questions 1–12

- You will hear part of a radio programme in which someone is talking about how to get a pay rise.
- As you listen, for questions **1–12**, complete the notes using up to **three** words or a number.
- You will hear the recording twice.

Some tips on how to get a pay rise

The Situation

You have to make **(1)** .... feel that you deserve a pay rise.

Mark

He had a **(2)** .... from another firm.

He tried hard to **(3)** .... correctly.

He didn't make demands, but he **(4)** ....

Simon

He recommends doing things which are not in your **(5)** ....

He spent some of his own time attending **(6)** .... and conferences.

Claire

She decided to improve her **(7)** ....

Suddenly, the quality of her work was noticed by **(8)** ....

She now gets paid **(9)** .... more than she used to.

Sarah

Her job consisted of helping with **(10)** .... tasks.

She made a list of her original **(11)** .... and the ones she had added.

She asked for more money and a new **(12)** ....

18

Part 2

Questions 13–22

- You will hear five people talking on the phone about a problem which has occurred at work.
- For each extract there are two tasks. For Task One, choose the type of problem which has occurred from the list **A–H**. For Task Two, choose the action each person is taking from the list **A–H**.
- You will hear the recording twice.

TASK ONE – TYPE OF PROBLEM

- For questions **13–17**, match the extracts with the types of problems, listed **A–H**.
- For each extract, choose the problem referred to.
- Write **one** letter (**A–H**) next to the number of the extract.

13 ....

14 ....

15 ....

16 ....

17 ....

A	wrong goods delivered
B	non-payment of account
C	lost cheque
D	missing package
E	damaged goods
F	staff misconduct
G	missed deadline
H	mistake in brochure

TASK TWO – ACTION

- For questions **18–22**, match the extracts with the action each person is taking, listed **A–H**.
- For each extract, choose the action to be taken.
- Write **one** letter (**A–H**) next to the number of the extract.

18 ....

19 ....

20 ....

21 ....

22 ....

A	arrange meeting
B	waive charge
C	issue warning
D	check records
E	offer discount
F	ask for report
G	send information
H	consult colleagues

Part 3

Questions 23–30

- You will hear part of a radio interview with a successful young businessman called Jonathan Elvidge.
- For each question **23–30**, mark **one** letter (**A**, **B** or **C**) for the correct answer.
- You will hear the recording twice.

23   Before he started The Gadget Shop, Jonathan

     A   did a business studies course.

     B   ran another company.

     C   worked in an office.

24   The idea for The Gadget Shop was the result of

     A   a suggestion made by a friend of Jonathan's.

     B   a lack of suitable gifts available in other shops.

     C   Jonathan's own attitude to shopping.

25   How did Jonathan get advice on starting a business?

     A   He did some research into what other people had done.

     B   He talked to friends in the local business community.

     C   He contacted people who already ran shops successfully.

26   What problem did he have when he opened his first shop?

     A   He couldn't afford to buy suitable premises.

     B   An arrangement to borrow money fell through.

     C   His business failed to qualify for government aid.

27   Jonathan says that in the early days of the business

     A   it was easy to sell a lot of goods.

     B   attracting the right customers was a problem.

     C   the profits he made were surprisingly high.

28 Jonathan made a beginner's mistake when he

   A chose one of the most expensive sites in the mall.

   B agreed immediately to pay the rent he was asked for.

   C accepted a sharp increase in the rent on his premises.

29 Jonathan's new partner wanted him to

   A enlarge the floor-space of his shop.

   B look for some additional outlets.

   C extend the range of goods he sold.

30 How does Jonathan feel about his latest venture?

   A He finds it exciting.

   B It makes him rather nervous.

   C He is confident of success.

You now have 10 minutes to transfer your answers to your Answer Sheet.

SPEAKING

(about 16 minutes)

Part 1 Interview (about 3 minutes)

Practise answering these questions:

- What's your name, please? How do you spell that?
- Where do you come from?
- Tell me a bit about (*name of city/region*). What's it like?
- What are the traditional industries of the city/region?
- Are they being replaced by any new, different industries?
- What do you do for a living?

Part 2 Mini-presentation (about 6 minutes)

Choose **one** of three topics, and prepare a short talk on it.

CANDIDATE A

> **A: Communication:** the importance of good communication skills in developing a career in any kind of business

> **B: Career planning:** how to decide when it is time to look for a new job

> **C: Finance:** how to keep overheads to a minimum in a large company

CANDIDATE B

> **A: Travel:** how to prepare for a first visit to a foreign country

> **B: Advertising:** the importance of using popular culture in advertising

> **C: Project management:** the importance of defining the scope of a project

Part 3 Collaborative task and discussion (about 7 minutes)

Practise discussing this task and the questions that come after it with your partner.

> **Bonus**
>
> Your company has achieved record profits and wishes to reward its employees with some kind of one-off gift or bonus. You have been asked to join a committee which will advise the Board of Directors on how this can best be done.
>
> Discuss and decide together:
> - which employees will be eligible to receive the bonus
> - what form it should take.
> - whether it should vary from employee to employee, and if so, according to what criteria.*

The third discussion point is used when three candidates take the test together.

Follow-up discussion questions

- How important is the salary in determining how much you enjoy your job?
- How important is it that salary structures and fringe benefit systems are transparent?
- What do you see as the key to keeping a workforce motivated?
- What can senior managers do to encourage high morale among more junior employees?

TEST TWO
READING
(1 hour)

Part 1

Questions 1–8

- Look at the statements below and at the five sections of an article about not being promoted on the opposite page.
- Which section (**A, B, C, D** or **E**) of the article does each statement **1–8** refer to?
- For each statement **1–8**, mark **one** letter (**A, B, C, D** or **E**) on your Answer Sheet.
- You will need to use some of these letters more than once.

Example:
0   Make sure you don't forget what your ambition is.

1   There are reasons why some people are promoted and others are not.

2   You may decide that you don't mind having a boring job.

3   Volunteer to do work someone else doesn't want to do.

4   You should make sure that you are regarded as being excellent at your work.

5   A great many people are keen to work in certain professions.

6   It is possible that you may have a desire to continue working at the same place for a great deal of time.

7   Don't be annoyed because you think that others do not deserve promotions they are given.

8   Decide at what point you will give up a boring job.

A
Glamour jobs

Who would not love to work in a glamorous profession? But if you want to enter the glitzy world of publishing, television or film you'll find the competition fierce. People hoping to break into such fields are often advised to start at the bottom and work their way up through 'career opportunities' which consist mainly of typing, photocopying and making coffee. These jobs may well give you a taste of life in your dream field, but it's easy to get stuck and miss your chance to shimmy up the golden ladder.

B
Left behind

It can be disheartening to see people being promoted ahead of you, but instead of begrudging them their success, use the opportunity to ask yourself some hard questions. Every organisation promotes a certain type of person. It may be something as simple as a way of dressing or as complex as a shared world view. Perhaps you are not in what the firm considers the winning mould. If this is the case, try not to take it personally; it says more about the organisation's culture than about you as an individual.

C
Choices

You now have three options. First, you could try to fit the mould. Think carefully how much this might cramp your own style. Second, you can try to change the organisation, if you are committed to it in the long term. Your final option is to learn all you can from your job and then find a work place where you are appreciated. In many fields, being known as someone who gets things done is the best qualification for a job. Guard your reputation by being a consummate professional.

D
Dealing with disappointment

Your own lowering expectations can be the most effective way of staying in a dead-end job. Everyone starts to value themselves less if they find their talents under-used. After a while, you start expecting not to be considered for a promotion. Then, when you are turned down, you start to think: 'Oh, the promotion wasn't so glamorous – maybe this job isn't so bad after all'. To avoid sinking self-worth, keep your career goal clearly in mind and set a time-limit on how long you will spend doing any job that is a means to an end.

E
Be positive

But it isn't all doom and gloom. There are still lots of jobs and lots of movement within the glamorous professions. The most important thing to remember is that you must take responsibility for your own career. Don't sit around waiting for a talent scout to elevate you to superstardom. Use your initiative. Do something that is not in your job description or find a job your boss loathes and ask if you can perform it. You will make a good impression and gradually your role will expand.

Part 2
Questions 9–14

- Read this text taken from an article about working in teams.
- Choose the best sentence from the opposite page to fill each of the gaps.
- For each gap **9–14**, mark **one** letter (**A–H**) on your Answer Sheet.
- Do not mark any letter more than once.
- There is an example at the beginning (**0**).

TEAM WORKING

Team building has always been important at work. However, the concept of the team is not static. (0) ..*H*.. But with organisations structured in new ways, and with new types of working, so new types of team have been developed.

'There's a whole new area of activity around team building,' according to Dianne Riley-Moore of the Industrial Society. It carried out a survey into team working and found that 86% of the 408 human resources managers questioned said their organisations were investing significantly more in team building. Moreover, one in ten employers spent up to half their training budget on team-related training. **(9)**...... There is now much more teleworking, homeworking and hot desking. Contrasting the new de-layered structures with the more traditional, Mrs Riley-Moore says: 'The concepts of team building have to be addressed in different ways. There are organisations which still have a fairly traditional structure. **(10)**...... In this situation, she says, the idea is to 'build a team collectively, focusing on a specific set of activities, say within a department or function, with everybody involved in achieving certain outcomes.'

Other organisations are changing their structures and looking at how to maintain a sense of being in a team when people are no longer so accessible to each other. **(11)**...... These are put together for the duration of a project and then dissolved. An individual may be a member of several project teams at once. Mrs Riley-Moore says that in this instance people need to develop transferable team-working skills which they can carry from one team to another. **(12)**...... They also have to accept personal responsibility. They have to move away from the idea that the leader is accountable for managing the work of the team to one in which individual team members are all accountable. To achieve this, one of the core building blocks is inter-personal skills – listening, questioning, giving feedback – with each member being able to put their ideas across effectively. **(13)**......

Andy Dickson, a training consultant, says: 'An individual might be working in any number of teams across an organisation. Often they are on project teams, created just for a few weeks or months. **(14)**...... So instead of doing that, giving individuals the ability to work in teams in general is a good idea.'

Example:

A	They have to understand better what being a team member means.
B	More often, it involves undertaking a number of brief tasks which can only be completed successfully if they use the necessary team skills.
C	Obviously it would be crazy to do a team building programme each time a team is formed.
D	Moreover, growing use is being made of teams to handle one-off assignments.
E	The growth in such activity is undoubtedly linked to corporate restructuring.
F	Another is having much more clarity about team objectives.
G	They look at team building in terms of enhancing performance and increasing understanding of individual roles and responsibilities.
H	The traditional team works together in one location and has a hierarchy or leader.

Part 3

Questions 15–20

- Read the following article about the behaviour of bosses and the questions on the opposite page.
- For each question **15–20**, mark **one** letter (**A**, **B**, **C** or **D**) on your Answer Sheet for the answer you choose.

Bosses are not just people who have bigger salaries or cars than the rest of us. They behave differently. In many sometimes subtle and often painful ways, they show you it is them rather than you who is in the driving seat. This power allows bosses to behave badly at employees' expense. The accumulation of humiliations for subordinates adds up to the status they feel. One ploy is not to answer employee calls for days. It takes relatively little time to make a quick call but often the excuse after two or three weeks is that the boss did not have time. This, and a battery of degrading actions, merely emphasise where the power lies. What that excuse is saying is that the boss did not have time for you. The boss may even add insult to injury and say: 'Did you phone? I'm sorry, I never got the message.' The contempt of one who has power is never more starkly shown than when the boss tells such a lie.

Bosses may set up a meeting and then either cancel it at the last minute or be very late. Not only are they often late for a meeting, they also leave early and often have little or no idea what the detail of the meeting is about. They sit cryptically in the corner for a minute and then leave. All of that is there to show you who it is who has the power and that your time and convenience are less important than this childish show. Often this is the result of insecurity or just a failure to learn good manners.

Being tough and unresponsive to people and their feelings, the boss assumes everyone else is as well. They may even imagine that people respond better to terror and threats than to encouragement and praise. That produces a penchant for abuse, attack and denigration. And that in turn will produce good work only from a narrow range of resilient and thick-skinned people.

But it is once you get into meetings that real power language starts. When you get face to face, body language really becomes unmistakably obvious and the assertions of power become easy and evident. Typically, during a lengthy and well-researched presentation you are giving, the boss might put up a hand, turn to someone else and say: 'Yes, I think we get the drift and I hear what you say. Now, John, I think you have one or two ideas which might help push this boat out.'

However, some support for bosses behaving badly comes in *48 Laws of Power* by Robert Greene and Joost Elffers. Law 43 in this book states that those who act with authority are more likely to be accepted as leaders. Keeping a distance rather than attempting to be chummy is vital if leaders wish to have the ability to inspire loyalty, fear or love. Those who pretend to be one of the crowd elicit contempt. While many see a boss's unpredictability as an abuse, Law 47 suggests: 'Those who succeed at the game are those who control the patterns and vary them at will, keeping people off balance while they set the tempo. The powerful vary their rhythms and patterns and learn to improvise.'

Consultant Jonathan Wilson says: 'Many of those we work for do not realise the difference between the exercise of power and bullying. Bosses behaving badly may work in the short term and even be tolerated, but in the end those bosses cut themselves off from the organisation and do not get any meaningful feedback. Also, those beneath them will be too frightened to do anything creative and only do to the letter what they are told. People are people and sometimes they behave badly and lose their tempers, but sustained bullying as a way of running an organisation is counter-productive.'

15 The writer uses the example of bosses not returning calls to illustrate

    A the fact that people change when they become bosses.
    B the bad behaviour that most bosses are unaware of.
    C the low regard that bosses have for employees.
    D the unpredictable way in which bosses behave.

16 The writer says in the second paragraph that when bosses attend meetings,

    A they make it clear that they resent having to do so.
    B they aim to create a certain impression.
    C their contribution often spoils the meeting.
    D their behaviour varies from meeting to meeting.

17 According to the writer, when bosses are tough and unresponsive

    A the attitudes of people working for them often change.
    B some employees feel they have to improve their performance.
    C some people working for them do not find this upsetting.
    D employees tend not to understand their intentions correctly.

18 The writer uses the example of a presentation to illustrate

    A the fact that bosses tend to disagree just for the sake of it.
    B how little bosses really know about the work their employees do.
    C the fact that bosses often come to the wrong conclusions.
    D how keen bosses are to be in control of certain situations.

19 In *48 Laws of Power*, the authors state that

    A many bosses would like to be more pleasant to employees.
    B many bosses do not realise their behaviour is unpredictable.
    C bosses who are friendly do not gain respect.
    D bosses are seldom given the credit they deserve.

20 Which of the following does Jonathan Wilson say about bosses' bad behaviour?

    A It is understandable to a certain extent.
    B It is caused by their desire to keep away from employees.
    C It takes a great many different forms.
    D It can cause employees to do their work badly.

Part 4

Questions 21–30

- Read the article below about technology in the workplace.
- Choose the correct word to fill each gap from **A**, **B**, **C** or **D** on the opposite page.
- For each question **21–30**, mark **one** letter (**A**, **B**, **C** or **D**) on your Answer Sheet.
- There is an example at the beginning (**0**).

THE DOMINANT MACHINES

Anyone who thinks that the (**0**) ..C.. between humans and computers have crumbled should listen to the experiences of a few help-line engineers. One caller, for instance, complained that his screen was (**21**) .... – during a power cut. Then there was the chap who couldn't make his floppy-disk drive work. When the engineer suggested closing the door, the caller got up and shut the office door.

Such legends emphasise the enduring culture gap between computer users and IT professionals. But as a recent survey proves, technology is now both (**22**) .... and ubiquitous in the workplace. The research, which (**23**) .... more than 400 managers, directors and chief executives across a broad range of sectors, has provided (**24**) .... evidence of the exploitation of technologies such as e-mail and the internet.

Among the good (**25**) .... cited by respondents are faster decision-making, the ability to extend into overseas markets, and being able to (**26**) .... workforces far more flexibly.

It is not all that rosy, though. Business communications technology is still (**27**) .... short of expectations and creating problems of its own. Common gripes (**28**) .... junk e-mail, poorly designed and badly maintained web sites, and the rapid rate at which equipment becomes (**29**) .... Software is seen as far too complex, making it time-consuming to learn and costly to maintain. And the ability to work from home or while travelling is seen as a double-edged sword. People welcome the flexibility but (**30**) .... the fact that they are unable to escape from the pressures of work, day or night.

Example:

	A	hurdles	B	hindrances	C	barriers	D	obstructions

0 A ☐ B ☐ C ■ D ☐

21	A	bare	B	plain	C	blank	D	vacant
22	A	indispensable	B	instrumental	C	incessant	D	inseparable
23	A	extended	B	covered	C	ranged	D	referred
24	A	novel	B	original	C	topical	D	fresh
25	A	items	B	respects	C	particulars	D	points
26	A	delegate	B	dispose	C	deploy	D	devolve
27	A	falling	B	coming	C	landing	D	running
28	A	count	B	include	C	incorporate	D	entail
29	A	terminal	B	extinct	C	obsolete	D	void
30	A	aggrieve	B	object	C	enrage	D	resent

Part 5

Questions 31–40

- Read the article below about writing a CV.
- For each question **31–40**, write **one** word in CAPITAL LETTERS on your Answer Sheet.

Example: `0 | I | T`

GET AHEAD OF THE JOB PACK

Writing a CV is tedious – it's time-consuming, requires careful planning and is difficult to do well. Unfortunately, **(0)**........ is also a necessity if you are looking to find employment. It is the main tool you have at your disposal when looking for an interview.

Most employers rarely put much time into reading CVs – they often have hundreds to wade through – so it is crucial to grab **(31)**........ attention instantly. Most employers want a CV that's short and to the point and has **(32)**........ tailored to the job in question. Career aims, what skills you have **(33)**........ offer and relevant work experience are the most important aspects and should be addressed first. Equally important, however, are a clear layout (don't clutter it by trying to squeeze in as **(34)**........ as possible), enthusiastic language and no spelling mistakes. And don't ever fold your CV or send it in crumpled. **(35)**........ good your qualifications and experience may be, a CV is as heavily judged on presentation as it **(36)**........ on content.

All CVs should be accompanied by a covering letter, which should be addressed to a named person, **(37)**........ than a job description or 'Dear Sir/Madam'. All the information you need to convey can be covered in three short paragraphs, detailing the job you are applying **(38)**........ , your skills and experience, and a brief explanation of your career aims. Often the covering letter is **(39)**........ that the employer will see. And always follow up the application. It is very important to chase up employers, **(40)**........ they often forget about CVs. A gentle reminder may get you the job.

Part 6

Questions 41-52

- Read the text below about company newsletters.
- In most of the lines **41-52**, there is one extra word. It is either grammatically incorrect or does not fit in with the sense of the text. Some lines, however, are correct.
- If a line is correct, write **CORRECT** on your Answer Sheet.
- If there is an extra word in the line, write **the extra word** in CAPITAL LETTERS on your Answer Sheet.
- The exercise begins with two examples (**0**) and (**00**).

Examples: 0 C O R R E C T
00 W H O

COMPANY NEWSLETTERS

0 In the demanding world of direct marketing and customer communications, many

00 businesses have one – the individual who appointed from the staff to produce the

41 company newsletter. For some, it is a trial that involves themselves hounding

42 colleagues to produce copy on the time. For others, it is a joyous career move that

43 bestows the awesome title 'editor'. The glossiest customer publications may remain

44 the preserve of big firms, but computers and colour printers mean so that even

45 small companies which once were relied on smudgy duplicated customer leaflets can

46 produce acceptable colour newsletters. In the pursuit of a customer loyalty and

47 getting new business, a publication that is well produced is viewed by many as

48 for carrying more marketing clout than simpler mailshots. Peter Waldron, partner

49 in a law firm, says that customers have come about to expect his company's

50 newsletter, which is produced by in-house and direct-mailed to 1,000 local business

51 people. 'It's important that a newsletter is including personal, an interesting read

52 and looks like smart,' he says. Some organizations, charities for instance, produce

low-budget but highly effective newsletters.

WRITING

(1 hour 10 minutes)

Part 1

Question 1

- The bar chart below shows turnover for the London, New York and Frankfurt stock exchanges over three years.
- Using the information in the chart, write a short **report** comparing performance on the three exchanges.
- Write **120–140** words on the Answer Paper.

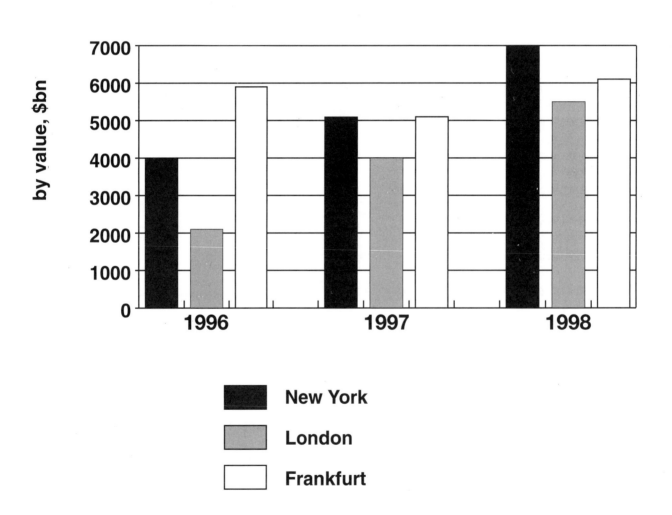

Part 2

Answer **ONE** of the questions 2, 3 or 4 below.

Question 2

- You work for a company which is growing rapidly. You and your colleagues are worried that the health and safety provisions which have been made for the office workers are becoming inadequate. The Human Resources Director has asked you to write a report outlining the concerns of the workforce.
- Write the **report**, recommending what action needs to be taken, and including the following points:
    - what dangers are caused by the design of the offices
    - whether procedures for dealing with emergencies are appropriate
    - how relevant skills and knowledge among the staff can be improved.
- Write **200–250** words on the Answer Paper.

Question 3

- Employees of the company you work for have for many years enjoyed substantial welfare benefits such as subsidised canteen lunches, free coffee and a programme of free social events for themselves and their families. Growing financial pressure on the company means that savings must be made. You have been asked by the Finance Director to write a proposal for revising the welfare benefit system.
- Write the **proposal**, describing the revised system and stating:
    - which benefits should be discontinued, which reduced and which retained
    - the reasons for these recommendations
    - the savings this would achieve.
- Write **200–250** words on the Answer Paper.

Question 4

- A business acquaintance of yours from a foreign company which is a client of the company you work for is about to spend several days visiting your company. You are organising the programme for this visit, but you yourself will not be available on the first day of the visit.
- Write a **fax** to your contact:
    - apologising for not being available when he/she arrives and explaining why this is so
    - outlining the programme you suggest for the visitor
    - offering some additional possibilities
    - giving brief details of practical arrangements such as transport and accommodation.
- Write **200–250** words on the Answer Paper.

Test Two   Listening

LISTENING
(about 40 minutes)

Part 1
Questions 1–12

- You will hear a recorded message left by a senior manager for his personal assistant.
- As you listen, for questions **1–12**, complete the notes using up to **three** words or a number.
- You will hear the recording twice.

Phone message – things to do

Senior Management meeting

Make amendments to the **(1)** ....

Sophie can help with any **(2)** ....

There is an appendix, which consists of a **(3)** ....

Remind people to deal with their **(4)** ....

Monday's appointments

The ten o'clock meeting has been **(5)** ....

Malcolm Vinall's number is **(6)** ....

Malcolm will need a parking place and a **(7)** ....

Re-schedule all **(8)** .... meetings for next week.

Less urgent matters

Book a room for the **(9)** .... meeting.

Begin to draw up the **(10)** .... for the meeting.

Ask Reprographics for copies of the **(11)** ....

The copies were due to be ready at the **(12)** ....

Part 2

Questions 13–22

- You will hear five people talking about the restructuring of the company they work for.
- For each extract there are two tasks. For Task One, choose the type of job each person does from the list **A–H**. For Task Two, choose the reaction each person has to the changes being made to the company from the list **A–H**.
- You will hear the recording twice.

TASK ONE – TYPE OF JOB

- For questions **13–17**, match the extracts with the types of jobs, listed **A–H**.
- For each extract, choose the job the speaker does.
- Write **one** letter (**A–H**) next to the number of the extract.

13 ....

14 ....

15 ....

16 ....

17 ....

A	secretary
B	shop floor worker
C	marketing assistant
D	receptionist
E	data input clerk
F	IT specialist
G	human resources assistant
H	finance manager

TASK TWO – REACTIONS TO THE CHANGES

- For questions **18–22**, match the extracts with the speakers' reactions, listed **A–H**.
- For each extract, choose the speaker's reaction to the changes being made to the company.
- Write **one** letter (**A–H**) next to the number of the extract.

18 ....

19 ....

20 ....

21 ....

22 ....

A	I don't think anything will really change.
B	I'm afraid of ageist attitudes.
C	I hope to be retrained.
D	I expect to be promoted.
E	I welcome the coming changes.
F	I plan to retire soon.
G	I'm afraid I'll be made redundant.
H	I think these changes are unnecessary.

Part 3

Questions 23–30

- You will hear part of a radio discussion on an issue concerning health at work. An expert called Sarah Baylis is being interviewed.
- For each question **23–30**, mark **one** letter (**A**, **B** or **C**) for the correct answer.
- You will hear the recording twice.

23 Poor health in the workforce is an important issue because

    A   the direct costs of ill health are rising fast.

    B   it is increasingly difficult to recruit new workers.

    C   it creates a wide range of direct and indirect costs.

24 Rates of absence are low in organisations in which

    A   employees are engaged in selling to the public.

    B   the workforce consists of healthcare professionals.

    C   there is a settled, mature workforce.

25 An estimate of the costs of absence to a typical company shows that

    A   the direct costs add up to more than the indirect costs.

    B   employing temporary cover raises costs and reduces productivity.

    C   the chief cost is the salary paid to the absent employee.

26 Early retirement as a result of poor health

    A   now costs companies more than they can afford.

    B   is something many older employees fear.

    C   is encouraged by recent changes in employment law.

27 The main reasons for absence from work are

    A   a small number of serious diseases.

    B   psychological as well as physical.

    C   not connected with poor health at all.

28 What can an employer do to control absence?

   A   target the employees who are absent most
   B   reduce the level of benefits paid to the workforce
   C   try to prevent the development of health problems

29 The example of a London hospital shows that

   A   health education can be part of the solution.
   B   for manual workers, the risk of injury is unavoidable.
   C   new technologies are the key to solving old problems.

30 According to Sarah, effective ways of managing absence in a company include

   A   introducing a medical insurance scheme for employees.
   B   changing the age of compulsory retirement.
   C   making continual checks on short-term absences.

You now have 10 minutes to transfer your answers to your Answer Sheet.

SPEAKING
(about 16 minutes)

Part 1 Interview (about 3 minutes)

Practise answering these questions:

- Could you give me your name, please?
- Do you have a job, or are you a student?
- Tell me about the course you're doing / your present job.
- What are your career aims and what qualifications will you need for that?
- What sorts of careers are most popular with young people in your country?
- In what ways do you expect your career to differ from your father's / mother's?

Part 2 Mini-presentation (about 6 minutes)

Choose **one** of three topics, and prepare a short talk on it.

CANDIDATE A

A: Customer relations: the importance of dealing promptly with customer dissatisfaction

B: Time management: how to prioritise tasks when returning to work after a week's absence

C: Recruitment: how to attract good staff in areas where there is a skills shortage

CANDIDATE B

> **A: Staff management:** how to deal with an employee who lacks motivation

> **B: Sales:** how to maintain team spirit among the members of a sales force

> **C: Health and safety:** the importance of regular checks and updates of health and safety procedures

Part 3 Collaborative task and discussion (about 7 minutes)

Practise discussing this task and the questions that come after it with your partner.

> **Moving office**
>
> Your department is going to have to move to new offices within the same building. There will be less space for each work-station than at present. Your Head of Department has asked you to help prepare your colleagues for the move.
>
> Discuss and decide together:
> - how to inform your colleagues of the move
> - what you will ask them to do before the move.
> - what you can do to encourage a positive attitude towards the coming changes.*

*The third discussion point is used when three candidates take the test together.

Follow-up discussion questions

- Why do employees often react to any proposed change by opposing it?
- What can be the result if coming changes are not discussed openly and prepared for adequately?
- To what extent should all staff be consulted before a change of this kind?
- How useful are formal structures such as a Staff Consultative Committee?

TEST THREE
READING
(1 hour)

Part 1

Questions 1–8

- Look at the statements below and at the five advertisements for jobs connected with sales on the opposite page.
- Which advert (**A, B, C, D** or **E**) does each statement **1–8** refer to?
- For each statement **1–8**, mark **one** letter (**A, B, C, D** or **E**) on your Answer Sheet.
- You will need to use some of these letters more than once.

Example:
0   This book is really about functioning in an international context.

1   Common beliefs are presented as if they were new ideas in this book.

2   People are referred to other sources for further information.

3   It would be a big mistake not to pay attention to the conclusions presented in this book.

4   This book covers certain difficult choices that have to be made.

5   This book mentions something that companies are particularly weak at.

6   This book's recommendations are based on the correct analysis of new requirements.

7   The information given in this book is not always consistent.

8   An example relevant to this book's subject is not included.

A

Business Process Redesign

The editors of this book have investigated how five managers coped with redesigning their companies' business processes and give first-hand accounts of how they lived through the experience and the subsequent organisational changes. Each case study is written by one of the key players on the project. A case study from a public sector organisation would have been useful and, because the book contains material from several authors, there are contradictions. However, this is more than compensated for by the insights gained from reading the case studies, which reveal so many lessons learnt the hard way.

B

The Global Manufacturing Vanguard

While this book concentrates on manufacturing, the real subject is true globalism – achieving common standards of excellence wherever a world-wide company operates. The examples are mainly automotive but apply generally. Globalism must be based on high efficiency, not low wages, is its message. Thus, one company featured has a thirty-strong top team and you can't join it without experience of at least three out of six areas and at least one international assignment. Although very readable, the book occasionally betrays inadequate breadth of knowledge and reporting. Its lessons can be ignored – but only at your peril.

C

Competing on the Edge

Business is not a controlled universe. Success in sport and management is analogous. Time is as crucial as money. The authors promulgate these now familiar insights as radical discoveries, but they do contribute relevant checklists and quizzes, plus clear guides to today's tricky management decisions, such as whether to 'adaptively innovate' (which can lead to the 'chaos trap') or to 'consistently execute' (which can result in the 'bureaucracy trap'). Named case histories are often frivolous and the dozen 'in-depth' studies are, oddly, anonymous. Nonetheless, this is a useful encyclopaedia of the new management.

D

The Management of Diversity

Essentially, this is a useful general guide to the subject of managing diversity. Current ideas and thinking about diversity are reviewed. The importance of valuing the differences between people and developing an inclusive workplace are emphasised. Related training and literature are listed for those readers interested in finding out more about the subject.

E

Intellectual Capital: The New Wealth of Organisations

The 'information society' has become a truism. Behind the clichés about the knowledge economy, company and worker, lies the reality that is reshaping the world – above all, the world of business. The author writes of 'the end of management as we know it'. His brilliant reportage delineates accurately how management must change to manage three varieties of intellectual capital: human (individual powers and resources), structural (accumulated knowledge and know-how of the organisation), and customer knowledge, 'probably the worst managed of all intangible assets'. This book is an asset in its own right.

Part 2

Questions 9–14

- Read this text taken from an article about performance appraisal.
- Choose the best sentence from the opposite page to fill each of the gaps.
- For each gap **9–14**, mark **one** letter (**A–H**) on your Answer Sheet.
- Do not mark any letter more than once.
- There is an example at the beginning (**0**).

APPRAISAL CAN BE TOLERABLE

Legal secretary Alice Speight was horrified when she entered her boss's office for her latest annual performance appraisal. 'To be honest, I hate doing these things and I don't really know how they work. Do you?' said her manager. Alice represents a third of the employees who recently responded to an Institute of Personnel and Development (IPD) survey by claiming their bosses treated appraisals as 'a bureaucratic chore'. **(0)** ..*H*..

'Appraisal systems have become very diverse during the last few years,' says Angela Edward, IPD's policy advisor. **(9)**...... For the person being appraised, that inability to take advantage of the opportunity they present may mean losing out on better pay, promotions and training.

At their simplest, performance appraisals enable employees to plan and control their work better, to learn from their mistakes and profit from their successes. **(10)**...... Max A Eggert, management psychologist and author of *The Managing Your Appraisal Pocketbook*, says: 'The first thing to do, for example, is to request a preliminary discussion about what is going to be assessed and what the results will be. **(11)**...... Will you need to produce any paperwork? Will the appraisal identify training needs or is it a chance to bargain for an increase in pay?'

In fact, the last decade has witnessed a clear trend away from connections between appraisals and pay. A recent study reveals that of the 77 per cent of British companies that have a formal appraisal system in place, almost half claim there is no link to money. **(12)**...... Instead, they only focus on the future of the staff member in terms of development needs.

(13)...... Almost a third of the IPD's survey respondents agreed that appraisal ratings have everything to do with how much your boss likes you and nothing to do with how well you do the job. But Angela Edward claims there is a solution: 'Insist on fairness. **(14)**...... Was that report late because you were incompetent, or did your manager omit to record the fact that you were given instructions to amend the whole thing at 10pm the night before it was due? Discuss details like this at length and make sure they are recorded.'

Example:

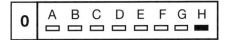

A   The result is that a great many managers – as well as their staff – don't really know how to make the most of them.

B   If there are complaints about your work or if you come fairly low on the appraisal scale system, ask why and demand examples.

C   In fact, the more untrained they are, the more frightened they may be of messing up.

D   What kind of questions will you be asked?

E   One problem that hasn't been easy to overcome is subjectivity.

F   Furthermore, steps have been taken in many organisations to ensure that appraisals have nothing to do with past performance.

G   Even if managers don't put a great deal of effort into this, there's a great deal people being appraised can do to help themselves.

H   Indeed, 15 per cent of managers said they would rather visit the dentist than carry out an appraisal.

Part 3

Questions 15–20

- Read the following article about focus groups and the questions on the opposite page.
- For each question **15–20**, mark **one** letter (**A**, **B**, **C** or **D**) on your Answer Sheet for the answer you choose.

Not only advertisers but even politicians and businesses are unable to make any decisions without first commissioning a series of focus groups. Focus group work is big business for market researchers – easily the most profitable work many do, with mark-up nicely proportioned to client wealth, not quality of work carried out. The focus group is far from new, dating back to the 1940s, when people were asked to discuss openly their reactions to a radio programme. Since then, they have been used primarily to discover consumer attitudes and motivation and to represent the views of particular groups and communities.

A typical focus group consists of a moderator questioning and listening to a group of individuals while they discuss a particular topic or react to a particular product. It usually lasts for one or two hours and ideally is conducted in a comfortable setting. This 'sensitive, qualitative' technique is akin to a think tank. Sessions can take on a life of their own, often revealing myriad unexpected outcomes. The moderator's tasks are to encourage and challenge, as well as manage, disrupt, divert and deal with other dynamics. Focus groups should ideally allow the moderator sufficient time and an appropriate setting to probe for and draw out important attitudes, perceptions, prejudices and opinions.

A group is typically composed of six to ten individuals who have something in common. The ideal is to run and run these groups until no novel information arises. This is, of course, potentially time-wasting and enormously expensive, because it is never clear when some new, worthwhile data arises. There also remains no consensus on how to 'play the group' – to make sure everyone has equal time to speak, to encourage or discourage disagreement or how to deal with dominant, distracting or dreary participants. In short, there are no clear guidelines of best practice, which is not good news for the person commissioning the focus group report.

The product of a focus group is usually a report, differing enormously in length, style and depth. They are characterised by having many quotes and by the essentially wry, perceptive interpretations of the observer on what, how and why ideas are generated. If the report writer is not the moderator, the long, jumbled, indeed often garbled notes need to be written up into a report. This, of necessity, involves interpretation, and highlighting and selecting core themes, major points of dissension and even implicit and badly articulated ideas. Precisely how reliable the interpretation is, is never clear.

Even the most skilful moderator cannot overcome the fundamental problems of groups making decisions. Some people have 'evaluation apprehension' – they self-censor, being scared to look foolish, so will never say in a public forum (the very open focus group) what they really think. Some go along for the spectacle and the free gifts, but contribute little, letting the garrulous speak for them. Therefore, focus group reports are biased towards the eloquent and opinionated, who might or might not speak for the group. Furthermore, it is difficult to think about something seriously when some know-all is continually talking. Focus groups allow little or no quiet time to think about the issue before being asked one's opinions. And finally, there are powerful conformity pressures to take sides and follow certain individuals or subgroups; in short to obey explicit or implicit upheld norms, giving a misleading idea of the spread of ideas in the group.

A few years ago, brainstorming groups were all the rage. The research on these groups showed that, despite what protagonists said, compared with the pooled ideas of people working alone, brainstorming groups nearly always produced fewer and lower-quality innovative ideas. Focus groups, being in many ways similar, share the same limitations.

15 The writer says in the first paragraph that focus groups

   A are more expensive for some clients than for others.
   B are chiefly relevant for understanding what consumers want.
   C are often forced on clients by market researchers.
   D are less reliable than they used to be.

16 The writer says in the second paragraph that the moderators of focus groups

   A should have an idea of likely outcomes before a session.
   B should make sure that the participants try to be objective.
   C should take little part in the discussion themselves.
   D should change the direction a discussion is taking.

17 Which of the following does the writer mention about focus groups in the third paragraph?

   A the lack of useful information that comes from them
   B the fact that they are not all carried out in the same way
   C the fact that they often take longer than was originally planned
   D the way in which common beliefs about them have changed

18 The writer says in the fourth paragraph that focus group reports

   A often try to make sessions sound more productive than they really were.
   B are often difficult to follow.
   C may involve a certain amount of guesswork.
   D sometimes concentrate on the least interesting aspects of the discussion.

19 Which of the following does the writer mention as a problem in the fifth paragraph?

   A the fact that some people give opinions they do not really hold
   B the tendency of some people to give opinions they know will cause argument
   C the fact that some people change their minds during sessions
   D the tendency of some people to talk about things they do not know much about

20 What does the writer imply about focus groups in the final paragraph?

   A They are not suited to certain types of business.
   B Research on them should not be taken too seriously.
   C People do not really enjoy taking part in them.
   D They are not likely to remain in fashion permanently.

Part 4
Questions 21–30

- Read the text below about the employment of older workers in Britain.
- Choose the correct word to fill each gap from **A**, **B**, **C** or **D** on the opposite page.
- For each question **21–30**, mark **one** letter (**A**, **B**, **C** or **D**) on your Answer Sheet.
- There is an example at the beginning (**0**).

OLDER WORKERS ARE JUST THE JOB

The existence of a 'lost generation' of unemployed older workers in Britain was **(0)**..*D*.. by recent government moves to encourage those aged over 50 to return to work. It is hoped that older people will add a valuable source of expertise to the labour **(21)**......, but how willing are employers to **(22)**...... those aged 50 or over? The employment agency MSL acknowledges that some firms are reluctant to do so.

'Many companies are looking for flexibility and a **(23)**......, to embrace change, which makes them look towards younger people who may have worked successfully for several employers **(24)**...... eight or ten years,' says MSL's Nick Marsh. 'Such staff will have shown themselves able to adapt to different business cultures. Managers in their forties or fifties may not fit this **(25)**......, perhaps having been with the same company for most of their working lives. Loyalty and commitment are no longer measured solely in **(26)**...... of length of service with a single employer.'

This attitude contrasts with a change of mind by management experts. They now recommend **(27)**...... on to experienced people, if only as a way of avoiding making old mistakes again. Several have acknowledged that the 'delayering' of a few years back may have **(28)**...... permanent harm to organisations by removing the older people, who could have passed on their accumulated techniques.

MSL says the challenge for the older manager in search of a new job is to match his or her experience as **(29)**...... as possible to stated requirements and to accentuate the positive, such as their **(30)**...... of knowledge, maturity in decision-making and calmness under pressure.

Example:

| | A pointed | B focused | C featured | D highlighted |

0 A B C D (D marked)

21 A mass   B group   C body   D force
22 A take on   B put up   C set about   D pick on
23 A preparation B willingness C consent   D mood
24 A along   B over   C across   D upon
25 A portrait   B sketch   C profile   D figure
26 A terms   B light   C grounds   D regard
27 A sticking   B keeping   C hanging   D carrying
28 A led   B done   C given   D made
29 A strictly   B securely   C finely   D closely
30 A length   B width   C height   D depth

Part 5

Questions 31–40

- Read the article below about public relations.
- For each question **31–40**, write **one** word in CAPITAL LETTERS on your Answer Sheet.

Example: **0** D O

PUBLIC RELATIONS AND SMALL COMPANIES

Making things is easy. Anyone can **(0)**........ that. It's selling them that's the problem. Sending round salesmen is one way of coping but a company needs publicity to reach beyond its salesmen's calls. **(31)**....... do that, you have to have a go at public relations.

What is public relations? **(32)**....... its simplest, it is the company's reputation and contact with the rest of the world. That means everything from the telephone switchboard to the warranty service. If it **(33)**....... several minutes for the company's telephone to be answered and the operator is off-hand and surly, customers will reckon they are dealing with an incompetent organisation. Similarly, **(34)**....... is little point in a retailer having a glamorous image if the sales assistants talk only to each other. Furthermore, producing messy and blurred brochures degrades the image. It costs little to change elementary but important things **(35)**....... as these in even very small companies. For instance, getting a professional designer to redo the letterhead and the company brochures can transform the image of **(36)**....... tiniest outfit.

Many companies are **(37)**....... small to have a full-time PR person, much less employ a consultancy. But that does not mean nothing can be done. Amateurs can do it perfectly well, as **(38)**....... as they are not amateurish. Indeed, the do-it-yourself approach can outdo the highly-paid professionals by asking the first question people paid by the hour often ignore: who are you trying to influence and **(39)**....... do you need to tell them? For example, if 100 buying managers make up 80% of your market, you can talk to **(40)**....... one individually.

Part 6
Questions 41–52

- Read the advertisement below for an editor.
- In most of the lines **41–52**, there is one extra word. It is either grammatically incorrect or does not fit in with the sense of the text. Some lines, however, are correct.
- If a line is correct, write **CORRECT** on your Answer Sheet.
- If there is an extra word in the line, write **the extra word** in CAPITAL LETTERS on your Answer Sheet.
- The exercise begins with two examples (**0**) and (**00**).

Examples: 0 ONE
00 CORRECT

EDITOR REQUIRED

0   The leading one magazine for the international broadcasting industry, is

00 looking to recruit an experienced editor. The ideal candidate will have at least four

41 years' journalism experience, with at least two years period in a senior editorial

42 role. The successful candidate will be a graduate, and will have to demonstrate

43 a proven track record of writing both news and feature articles in English, if

44 preferably on a media-related publication. However, consideration will also be given

45 to candidates but with no direct knowledge of the media or television sectors. You

46 will have to combine with management skills, journalistic flair and a sense of

47 humour in the face of tight deadlines and a demanding international travel schedule.

48 Based in the capital, and you will enjoy being part of a well-respected, enthusiastic,

49 young and dynamic group of these professionals. The position offers an excellent

50 salary and above benefit package. If you feel you would enjoy the challenges and the

51 many rewards this position brings, please send a brief resumé together with a

52 covering letter explaining why that you should be considered for the position.

Test Three Writing

WRITING
(1 hour 10 minutes)

Part 1

Question 1

- The graph below shows circulation figures for three teenage magazines, called *Magic*, *Sparks* and *Wavy*, over a five-year period.
- Using the information in the graph, write a short **report** comparing the performance of the three magazines.
- Write **120–140** words on the Answer Paper.

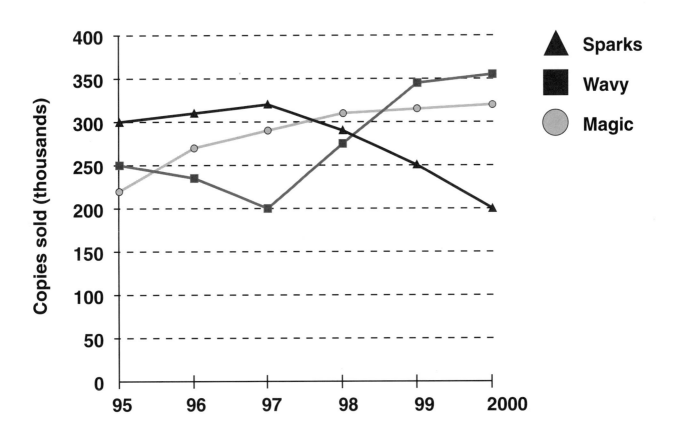

Part 2

Answer **ONE** of the questions 2, 3 or 4 below.

Question 2

- Your company recently had a stand at an annual trade fair in a foreign country. You attended the fair and helped to staff the stand. Your manager has asked you to write a brief report on the event.
- Write the **report**, summarizing your experience of attending this event, and commenting on the following:
    - the size and range of the trade fair
    - the position which your company's stand was given
    - the level of interest in the stand
    - whether future participation by your company in this trade fair is desirable, and if so, what changes should be made next time.
- Write **200–250** words on the Answer Paper.

Question 3

- You work in a large open-plan office, where each employee has only a small work-station, and noise is a problem. No additional space is available, but your group manager has asked you to draw up a proposal, suggesting some ways of improving the situation.
- Write the **proposal**, giving a brief outline of the problem and considering the following ideas:
    - whether to impose rules, for example, on having coffee breaks in the office
    - whether to introduce a system of more flexible hours of work
    - how changes in the office layout and furniture could help
    - whether a system of working from home could be introduced for some kinds of staff.
- Write **200–250** words on the Answer Paper.

Question 4

- Your company is about to take on a number of new trainees. A preliminary selection has already taken place, and the short-listed applicants will be invited to spend a day touring parts of the company, and participating in tests and interviews. You have been asked to draft a letter to them.
- Write the **letter** to the short-listed applicants:
    - inviting them to attend
    - outlining the programme for the day
    - explaining how they should prepare for their visit
    - giving details of how to get to the company's premises.
- Write **200–250** words on the Answer Paper.

Test Three   Listening

LISTENING
(about 40 minutes)

Part 1

Questions 1–12

- You will hear the organiser of an international conference welcoming delegates to the final day, and giving details of the programme.
- As you listen, for questions **1–12**, complete the notes using up to **three** words or a number.
- You will hear the recording twice.

Conference delegates – notes and reminders

General

A camera and a **(1)** .... have been lost.

People can get **(2)** .... if they missed them yesterday afternoon.

Everyone should fill in a **(3)** .... and leave it in reception.

A list of contact details such as **(4)** .... is being compiled.

The conference has made some useful **(5)** .... possible.

Leaving arrangements

At 5 o'clock the **(6)** .... will arrive.

Those leaving tomorrow must be out of their rooms by **(7)** ....

All **(8)** .... must be taken down today.

Today's programme

Anne Kramer will lead a **(9)** .... at 11.30.

It will now take place in the **(10)** ....

This afternoon there is a presentation on getting **(11)** .... for SMEs.

This evening, a **(12)** .... has been arranged.

Part 2
Questions 13-22

- You will hear five people talking about the services their small firms provide to a large company.
- For each extract there are two tasks. For Task One, choose the type of service each firm provides from the list **A-H**. For Task Two, choose the special advantage of the service each firm offers, from the list **A-H**.
- You will hear the recording twice.

TASK ONE – TYPE OF SERVICE

- For questions **13-17**, match the extracts with the types of services, listed **A-H**.
- For each extract, choose the service provided by the speaker's small firm.
- Write **one** letter (**A-H**) next to the number of the extract.

13 ....

14 ....

15 ....

16 ....

17 ....

A	courier service
B	cleaning
C	office equipment maintenance
D	temporary office staff
E	security
F	staff training
G	car hire
H	office equipment hire

TASK TWO – SPECIAL ADVANTAGE

- For questions **18-22**, match the extracts with the special advantages of the services, listed **A-H**.
- For each extract, choose the special advantage of the service offered.
- Write **one** letter (**A-H**) next to the number of the extract.

18 ....

19 ....

20 ....

21 ....

22 ....

A	attention to detail
B	flexibility of approach
C	good value for money
D	innovative approach
E	speed of response
F	high calibre of personnel
G	wide range of services
H	reliability of personnel

Part 3
Questions 23–30

- You will hear part of a job interview. A Human Resources officer, James, and a manager, Anna, are interviewing Karen for the post of P.A. to Anna.
- For each question **23–30**, mark **one** letter (**A**, **B** or **C**) for the correct answer.
- You will hear the recording twice.

23 After she left school, Karen

    A did several jobs before becoming a student.

    B went to teacher training college.

    C decided to look for a job in another country.

24 In her last job, one of her duties was to

    A deal with enquiries.

    B supervise other staff.

    C arrange meetings.

25 She left her last job because she felt that

    A it was the right time to move on.

    B she was losing interest in the work.

    C she might be made redundant.

26 She decided to apply for this job because of

    A the contrast with her previous post.

    B the opportunities it offers for career development.

    C the higher level of responsibility it involves.

27 The post of P.A. to Anna may involve

    A some use of foreign languages.

    B helping to entertain clients.

    C a limited amount of overseas travel.

28 Which of these is definitely part of the job?

- **A** attending meetings
- **B** filing correspondence
- **C** writing reports

29 What does Karen see as her main strength?

- **A** She is always calm in a crisis.
- **B** Other people can rely on her.
- **C** She reacts quickly to sudden events.

30 Karen asks for more information about

- **A** the starting date for the post.
- **B** the point she would be at on the salary scale.
- **C** the hours she would have to work each day.

You now have 10 minutes to transfer your answers to your Answer Sheet.

Test Three Speaking

SPEAKING
(about 16 minutes)

Part 1 Interview (about 3 minutes)

Practise answering these questions:

- What's your surname? And your initial?
- What kind of business are you (planning to be) involved in?
- What do you like doing best in your spare time?
- Which leisure activities are most popular with young people in your country?
- How do people normally travel to work in your city / region?
- Do you expect international travel to be a necessary part of your career? Would you welcome that?

Part 2 Mini-presentation (about 6 minutes)

Choose **one** of three topics, and prepare a short talk on it.

CANDIDATE A

> **A: Communication:** the importance of ensuring that e-mail and internet services are used efficiently at work

> **B: Management:** how to make successful use of temporary staff contracts

> **C: Product promotion:** the importance of promoting a product appropriately to the age-group it is aimed at

CANDIDATE B

> **A: Skills:** how to check a job applicant's skills quickly and effectively

> **B: Technology:** the importance of new technology in selling products

> **C: Training:** how to ensure that money spent on staff training is a good investment

Part 3 Collaborative task and discussion (about 7 minutes)

Practise discussing this task and the questions that come after it with your partner.

> **New division**
>
> Your company is growing fast, and a new division has just been formed. Most of the personnel are new to the company, and you have been asked to suggest some ways of helping them to bond with each other in order to form an effective team.
>
> Discuss and decide together:
> - why workplace bonding is so important
> - what techniques or events you would recommend in order to encourage the process.
> - how to ensure that everyone is included in the process.*

*The third discussion point is used when three candidates take the test together.

Follow-up discussion questions

- Why are the social aspects of their working lives so important to people?
- How can the success of a company be affected by personal relationships among its staff?
- How much attention should a company pay to this matter in terms of time and money?
- Should a company have any right to interfere in what employees choose to do with their free time?

TEST FOUR

READING

(1 hour)

Part 1

Questions 1–8

- Look at the statements below and at the five advertisements for jobs connected with sales on the opposite page.
- Which advert (**A, B, C, D** or **E**) does each statement **1–8** refer to?
- For each statement **1–8**, mark **one** letter (**A, B, C, D** or **E**) on your Answer Sheet.
- You will need to use some of these letters more than once.

Example:
0   Managers do not want to leave the other person depressed about what they have told them.

1   Managers should decide what they want to achieve from talking to the other person.

2   Managers sometimes tell themselves things which they realise are not true.

3   The other person is very likely to deny an accusation a manager makes.

4   The other person is likely to change their attitude to what they have been told.

5   Managers should be careful not to talk nonsense when criticising the other person.

6   Managers frequently fail to pay attention to an important part of criticising others.

7   Managers should make it clear that they are not being as severe as they could be.

8   People expecting bad news are still surprised by it.

A. Uncertainty

Most managers hate confrontations and are unsure of how to handle them when they need to. In consequence, unpleasant situations become something to be postponed indefinitely. Most of us put off warning people, reprimanding people or firing people for far longer than we should. We invent rationalisations we know to be unreal. We wait to be chivvied by our bosses into tackling unpleasant situations. If you never have to be chivvied, you'll create an excellent impression that can benefit your career.

B. Preparation

Before undertaking such tasks, however, the first essential, too often neglected, is to brief yourself thoroughly. Almost always, the person to be reprimanded will refute your criticism and may well have thought more, and know more about it all than you. Have specific details, not generalities, at your fingertips. Never say: 'You are often late back from lunch.' Say instead: 'You have been more than half an hour late back from lunch seven times in the last three weeks.' If you rely on generalities, your case will be weakened, perhaps totally undermined, and the dispute will degenerate into petulance.

C. A Hard Job

Once briefed, you must define the objectives of the confrontation. Generally, unless it is a termination interview, you will not want to demotivate the person. On the contrary, you will usually be seeking to remotivate them. You will be keen that he or she accepts what you have to say but does not go away utterly downcast or disheartened. This is extremely difficult to achieve, but it can be done. For a start, be at pains to be fair. Let it be known that you could easily be more critical but have no wish to be too harsh.

D. Good Advice

There are other good ways of handling confrontations. Firstly, control your non-verbal communication. Without minimising the seriousness of the situation, smile as often as possible. Secondly, start with a simple statement. Nerves can make even the most articulate person gibber on such occasions, with disastrous results. When you open your mouth to censure someone, make sure you don't put your own foot in it. And thirdly, seek agreement. Without bullying, try hard to get the person to state his or her agreement to what you have been saying. Someone who is unwilling to agree in your presence will most likely be harbouring resentments.

E. A Special Situation

Of course, some of the above are unnecessary, indeed irrelevant, if the other person is being fired. However much they may have been anticipating it, being fired always comes as a shock. Human beings have an extraordinary capacity to carry contradictory thoughts in their minds. Even though they know being fired is on the cards, they will not want to imagine it happening. After they have left, they will be embittered. No matter how reasonable their initial reaction, they will soon, understandably, build up a welter of resentment and possibly consult lawyers.

Part 2
Questions 9–14

- Read this text taken from an article about relationship marketing, or one-to-one marketing.
- Choose the best sentence from the opposite page to fill each of the gaps.
- For each gap **9–14**, mark **one** letter (**A–H**) on your Answer Sheet.
- Do not mark any letter more than once.
- There is an example at the beginning (**0**).

ONE-TO-ONE MARKETING

After an initial wave of enthusiasm, relationship marketing is starting to get a bad press. The basic idea is seductive. **(0)** ..*H*.. A good way of retaining them seems to be recognising that they exist, communicating with them, and responding to the need they express through this dialogue.

The trouble is that real relationship marketing, or one-to-one marketing, as some people call it, is awesomely difficult. **(9)**...... Many would-be relationship marketers fail to do so. Some have been seduced by opportunists who hijack the phraseology to sell old ideas. Others have simply done it badly.

In some markets, such as airlines, a tiny proportion of customers accounts for a huge percentage of revenue and profits. In other markets, such as bookselling, the value of each customer tends to be more equal because virtually every bookshop's customers have different needs. Few of them all want the same books. But the needs of airline travellers tend to be pretty similar, and therefore products and services can easily be customised. **(10)**......

Furthermore, interaction is very difficult. The company has to communicate with each customer in a way that recognises their specific needs and characteristics and persuades them to respond. Customer response then helps the company's marketers learn still more about their customers' needs and wishes. **(11)**......

For relationship marketing to work, a customer needs to be 'recognised' no matter how, when or where they 'touch' the company, whether it's a phone call to sales, a letter querying an invoice, a faxed complaint to customer services, or a website visit. This means that companies must have enterprise-wide customer information systems. **(12)**...... And such data should be instantly available to any member of staff who needs it.

Why do some attempts at relationship marketing fail? **(13)**...... In most businesses, this is such that they are built around functional departments or processes. The key is how to build the organisation around the customer. This involves customising the service to reflect the specific desires of the customer. **(14)**...... But that is easier said than done.

Example:

- **A** So some businesses lend themselves to one-to-one marketing far more than others.

- **B** But while it's all very well finding out about your customers in this way, what are you going to do with the information?

- **C** After all, relationship marketing is a pointless task unless the customer actually sees these being satisfied.

- **D** The problem is not really the systems, but the culture.

- **E** It indicates that there are very few companies who have an inkling about how to create good relationships with customers.

- **F** These are created to gather all relevant information, including a history of all dealings with each customer.

- **G** The fact is that, for most established companies, achieving the perfect one-to-one relationship is a formidable task.

- **H** We all know that money invested in keeping customers is more productive than money spent trying to replace ones we have lost.

Part 3

Questions 15–20

- Read the following article about consultancy and the questions on the opposite page.
- For each question **15–20**, mark **one** letter (**A**, **B**, **C** or **D**) on your Answer Sheet for the answer you choose.

'Businesslike' and 'professional' are two of the most abused descriptions in working life. Even at the most senior management levels, where you would have thought they would all know better, and at least have learnt some of the tricks of the trade, the message that comes over loud and clear in many companies is: this organisation is rife with conflict and dysfunctional relationships. As a result, the business is being affected because, to put it at its most crude, senior managers just do not get on.

For consultants this has proved something of a gold mine. For whenever there is a problem, be it business or management, the outsider can soon find that it really all comes down to conflict between the very parties who are being paid, often very well, to solve the problem which they are in fact creating. Successful conflict resolution is at the heart of management consultancy, not least because all change must revolve around overcoming resistance and making sure everyone is not only facing the same way and understanding where they are going, but that they also understand how they fit into the overall picture.

So why is it that people who have a vested interest in getting along – after all, their bonuses and wage packets depend on it – and are highly skilled, articulate, well trained and experienced, are often in a very immature conflict? Consultant Wendy Clark says: 'At the root of the problem is the fact that work throws together lots of people who normally would have nothing to do with each other. Also, it puts these potentially inimical people in an artificial situation. On top of that, the organisation speaks in double talk. While the official line may be all about co-operation, collaboration and team work, what the unwritten rules and working culture are all about are pushing others aside, exploiting weakness, talking loud, refusing to listen and winning or losing. No one can totally eradicate the hidden culture. What the consultant can try to do is make everyone a bit more adult and mature; if you like, to start using the emotional capital more effectively.'

Like much of consultancy, in black and white it all looks very easy. After all, what you are trying to do is to get sophisticated, intelligent people to talk honestly to each other and to communicate on the level. As consultant Brian Langham says: 'In senior teams it's all about power and conflicting agendas. What you have to do is get the various sides to negotiate a team position. Somehow you have to get away from I-win-you-lose to a win-win position where both feel they are on the team.' Consultant Peter Renwick says: 'The object is not to change personalities but to change behaviour, and the most deep-seated behaviour can be changed if managers are honest and level with each other. When things are left unsaid and managers beat about the bush, matters only get worse.' However, no two consultants sell exactly the same line. Consultant Bridget Skelton says: 'I see our role as taking the personal emotion usually caused by insecurities out of the argument and replacing this with business arguments. Debate is healthy but it has to be sensible and logical debate aimed at improving shareholder value, not protecting someone who is worried about the future.'

Sometimes even the most inspired consultant finds that positions have become too entrenched, emotions too sour and the conflict too ingrained to change. That is when the consultant's little helper, sacking people, comes in. If one or two people are taken out of any team and everyone moved around even slightly, the chemistry can change dramatically and with it the chance to get businesspeople and professionals to act in a way more worthy of their titles.

15 In the first paragraph, the writer expresses surprise that senior managers

- **A** allow personal relationships to interfere with their work.
- **B** are held in low regard by others in their organisations.
- **C** expect personal relationships at work to be difficult.
- **D** apply what they have learnt in inappropriate ways.

16 The writer says in the second paragraph that consultants have to deal with

- **A** people who believe they know better how to resolve conflict in the workplace.
- **B** people who want to make major changes to the organisation they work for.
- **C** people who believe they are more influential at work than they really are.
- **D** people who themselves should be putting an end to conflict in the workplace.

17 Wendy Clark believes that one reason for conflict is that

- **A** organisations believe it brings out the best in people.
- **B** people are made to feel that they should pursue selfish objectives.
- **C** organisations place too much emphasis on team work.
- **D** people tend to be more immature at work than away from it.

18 Consultants Brian Langham and Peter Renwick both refer to

- **A** how hard it is for consultants to resolve conflict.
- **B** how keen many managers are to resolve conflict.
- **C** the causes of conflict at work.
- **D** the inevitability of conflict at work.

19 Bridget Skelton's approach differs from that of Brian and Peter in that

- **A** she does not try to be neutral during discussions.
- **B** she believes a certain amount of conflict is desirable.
- **C** she does not believe that emotion is the real cause of conflict.
- **D** she focuses purely on the commercial results of conflict.

20 The writer concludes in the final paragraph that

- **A** getting a consultant to resolve conflict is often a waste of time.
- **B** it may be necessary to put the blame for conflict on certain individuals.
- **C** sometimes threats are the only way of resolving conflict.
- **D** minor changes can cause people in conflict to become friendly with each other.

Part 4
Questions 21–30

- Read the article below about developments in employment in Britain.
- Choose the correct word to fill each gap from **A, B, C** or **D** on the opposite page.
- For each question **21–30**, mark **one** letter (**A, B, C** or **D**) on your Answer Sheet.
- There is an example at the beginning (**0**).

FOCUS ON THE FUTURE OF WORK

The future of paid employment in Britain is the (0)...A... of much debate. Some commentators assert that the nature of work is changing in fundamental ways. They highlight the scale and scope of recent technological innovations, the forces of globalisation and the pattern of corporate restructuring, and (21)....... an even more dramatic transformation in the forms of paid and unpaid work, and the boundaries between work, leisure and family life. And they point to current changes in hours of work and (22)....... of security – for example, the increased use of fixed-term contracts and temporary work.

In recent times, there has been an increase in (23)....... of female participation in paid, predominantly part-time, employment and a (24)....... in full-time manual job opportunities for men. These developments have important implications, not only for the performance of the paid workforce, but also for the (25)....... of labour in the household and the provision of childcare facilities.

Taking the question of performance in the workplace, relevant issues include: how, if at all, increased female participation will (26)....... on the work environment, and whether women are (27)....... into the paid workforce as primary or secondary earners.

(28)....... about decreasing opportunities for secure careers and 'jobs for life' has intensified following recent high-profile examples of company reorganisation, downsizing and outsourcing. Is this a major and lasting (29)....... in patterns of employment? What are the social and economic consequences within the household of uncertain careers? As organisations downsize, multi-skilling and work flexibility become (30)........ . But who is responsible for training in the necessary skills: employers, the state or the individual?

Example:

    A subject   **B** case   **C** field   **D** aspect

0	A ■	B ☐	C ☐	D ☐

21	**A** reckon	**B** anticipate	**C** deem	**D** conceive
22	**A** grades	**B** ranks	**C** levels	**D** classes
23	**A** extents	**B** scales	**C** degrees	**D** rates
24	**A** deterioration	**B** decay	**C** decline	**D** depreciation
25	**A** separation	**B** share	**C** division	**D** ratio
26	**A** impact	**B** bear	**C** weigh	**D** impress
27	**A** integrated	**B** mingled	**C** unified	**D** harmonised
28	**A** Theory	**B** Estimation	**C** Notion	**D** Speculation
29	**A** variation	**B** amendment	**C** shift	**D** turn
30	**A** principal	**B** crucial	**C** foremost	**D** prime

Part 5
Questions 31–40

- Read the text below about tests that are used for assessing job candidates.
- For each question **31–40**, write **one** word in CAPITAL LETTERS on your Answer Sheet.

Example: | 0 | A | N | D |

PSYCHOMETRIC TESTS

Picture yourself at a strange desk, with a questionnaire in front of you, a clock ticking loudly away, **(0)**......... your career prospects hanging on the answers you give with the pen held in your trembling hand. Welcome to the world of psychometric testing, **(31)**........ your personality will be laid bare for all – except you – to analyse.

Psychometric testing in the jobs market caught on in the 1980s. Traditional face-to-face interviews were increasingly seen **(32)**........ unreliable, relying on the subjective judgement of the interviewer, and working against those **(33)**........ had all the right qualifications for the job but turned into red-faced sweaty wrecks **(34)**........ moment they stumbled into an interview room.

Psychometric tests were introduced as a way **(35)**......... taking the guesswork out of employing staff. By the 1990s, they had become a multi-million pound business. Not only **(36)**........ a sizeable majority of companies introduce tests to recruit and appraise staff, but many even set **(37)**....... their own in-house assessment centres run by professional psychologists. If you apply for a job nowadays with a medium to large organisation, you stand a 75% chance of **(38)**....... tested in some way.

Critics of psychometric tests believe they put too **(39)**....... pressure on job applicants. Many of us fill in questionnaires in magazines, but while it's fun to learn how you score in this kind of test, it's quite **(40)**....... thing to be confronted with a personality review that's backed by scientific data and research, especially when your career prospects depend on the results.

Part 6
Questions 41–52

- Read the article below about training.
- In most of the lines **41–52**, there is one extra word. It is either grammatically incorrect or does not fit in with the sense of the text. Some lines, however, are correct.
- If a line is correct, write **CORRECT** on your Answer Sheet.
- If there is an extra word in the line, write **the extra word** in CAPITAL LETTERS on your Answer Sheet.
- The exercise begins with two examples (**0**) and (**00**).

Examples: 0 W H A T
00 C O R R E C T

BUYING TRAINING

0 Training must be tailored specifically to what needs. It should take account of the

00 requirements not only of the industry but also of the corporate culture and specific

41 tasks involved in. So before choosing any training company, talk to recent clients.

42 Ask especially what was more they could have got out of the training company.

43 Does the trainer do off-the-shelf work or with more tailor-made courses? Does it

44 focus on the latest fad, or therefore sell out-of-date and inappropriate tools? The

45 most important part of training is the design stage. That identifies out the gap

46 between how things are and how you would like them to be. That gap represents

47 the difference between how the organisation is performing and how else it should be

48 performing, what people can do and what they should be able to do. People often

49 buy training because they should believe it is a good thing. Before you engage a

50 training company, you should be clear as about what you are trying to achieve and

51 how the training will benefit to the organisation. Otherwise, don't bother. There are

52 plenty of more effective ways in which you can even spend your company's money.

Test Four Writing

WRITING

(1 hour 10 minutes)

Part 1

Question 1

- The bar chart below shows the pattern of sales of men's and women's clothes made by *Fitz*, a UK-based chain of clothes shops, over a one-week period.
- Using the information in the chart, write a short **report** comparing the pattern of sales for men's clothes with that for women's clothes.
- Write **120–140** words on the Answer Paper.

Part 2

Answer **ONE** of the questions 2, 3 or 4 below.

Question 2

- Some complaints have recently been made about some employees of your company regarding their attitude to external telephone callers and visitors. The speed of response, helpfulness and politeness of staff have all been criticised. Your manager has asked you to investigate these complaints and write a report on the situation.
- Write the **report**, describing the problem and including the following points:
    - which kinds of staff are affected most by this issue
    - whether any disciplinary action or monitoring is necessary
    - what sort of training could be offered to key staff
    - what general guidelines should be given to all employees.
- Write **200–250** words on the Answer Paper.

Question 3

- You have been in your present post for several years, and have reached a point where you feel bored and frustrated. Unless you can develop the post in some new direction, you feel that you should look for a new job. Your line manager is supportive, and has asked you to write a proposal showing how the post could be developed.
- Write the **proposal**, outlining the situation and referring to the following:
    - the aspects of your post which you believe could be developed
    - details of any training you would need
    - how your present duties would be covered
    - the benefits this would bring to the company.
- Write **200–250** words on the Answer Paper.

Question 4

- You have learned through a business contact that another company is developing a new product which may be in competition with something in your company's current product range. You are concerned about this and have decided to e-mail a senior colleague with whom you work closely.
- Write the **e-mail**:
    - explaining the circumstances in which you got this information
    - describing everything you know about the rival product
    - comparing it with your company's product and explaining why it could be a threat
    - suggesting what you should do next.
- Write **200–250** words on the Answer Paper.

LISTENING
(about 40 minutes)

Part 1
Questions 1–12

- You will hear part of a presentation about the business services offered by a chain of hotels.
- As you listen, for questions **1–12**, complete the notes using up to **three** words or a number.
- You will hear the recording twice.

Elite Hotels

General

All Elite hotels are near important cities or at **(1)** ………………………….

They can cater for large events, such as a conference or product **(2)** ………………………….

The maximum number of people they arrange events for is **(3)** ………………………….

Conference and training suites

These suites provide a **(4)** …………………………. which is kept separate from tourist areas.

In the reception areas, fax and **(5)** …………………………. facilities are provided.

The **(6)** …………………………. of the meeting rooms means that they can be used for different kinds of meetings.

All meeting rooms have overhead projectors and **(7)** …………………………. in them.

Staying overnight

The twenty-four-hour package includes **(8)** …………………………. for partners of conference delegates.

For guests who want to work in the evening, bedrooms have desks and **(9)** ………………………….

Most hotels in this group have a **(10)** …………………………. which guests can use.

Booking

You can use Elite's free **(11)** …………………………. service to arrange your meeting.

The **(12)** …………………………. bill policy means you don't pay if things go wrong.

Part 2
Questions 13–22

- You will hear five people talking about courses they have been on at work.
- For each extract there are two tasks. For Task One, choose the title of the course each person has been on from the list **A–H**. For Task Two, choose the criticism of the course that each person expresses from the list **A–H**.
- You will hear the recording twice.

TASK ONE – TYPE OF COURSE

- For questions **13–17**, match the extracts with the titles of courses, listed **A–H**.
- For each extract, choose the course the speaker has been on.
- Write **one** letter (**A–H**) next to the number of the extract.

13 ……………….

14 ……………….

15 ……………….

16 ……………….

17 ……………….

A	Health and Safety Regulations
B	Time Management
C	Handling Conflict in the Workplace
D	Introducing Computer Graphics
E	Basic Business Statistics
F	Staff Selection Procedures
G	Welcome to the Internet
H	Improving Communication at Work

TASK TWO – CRITICISM

- For questions **18–22**, match the extracts with the criticisms made of the courses, listed **A–H**.
- For each extract, choose the criticism made.
- Write **one** letter (**A–H**) next to the number of the extract.

18 ……………….

19 ……………….

20 ……………….

21 ……………….

22 ……………….

A	poor presentation
B	too intensive
C	not practical enough
D	at an inconvenient time
E	too specialized
F	not demanding enough
G	not necessary
H	too short

Test Four   Listening

Part 3
Questions 23–30

- You will hear part of a radio programme called 'Ask an Expert'. A management consultant called Leo McBride is being interviewed.
- For each question **23–30**, mark **one** letter (**A**, **B** or **C**) for the correct answer.
- You will hear the recording twice.

23 What does Leo think about large companies?

    A   Some companies are now too large to manage.

    B   A well-run company can never be too big.

    C   Size is still the most important indicator of success.

24 According to Leo, if a company has a big market capitalisation,

    A   it is protected from attempts to take it over.

    B   it attracts take-over bids from growing companies.

    C   there is a tendency for it to grow too quickly.

25 Leo says that market capitalisation

    A   is usually better in larger companies.

    B   depends on size rather than performance.

    C   may be equal in companies of different sizes.

26 Leo thinks that, in a global economy

    A   a small company may be stronger than a large one.

    B   large companies normally perform better than small ones.

    C   what counts is having the right kinds of assets.

27 In Leo's opinion, in global capital markets

    A   it is becoming easier to find a way to beat your competitors.

    B   skills and knowledge are an important form of capital.

    C   increasingly high levels of investment are necessary.

28 According to Leo, advances in digital technology mean that

    A   cutting labour costs is a priority for most companies.

    B   a more extensive customer base has become necessary.

    C   a company does not need a wide range of activities.

29 What sorts of activities does Leo think a company should outsource?

    A   those for which there is a lack of in-house expertise

    B   those which are least profitable for the company

    C   those which can be done by unskilled workers

30 What does Leo think about adding further areas of specialisation?

    A   It is something all companies should aim to do.

    B   For most companies, the risks outweigh the benefits.

    C   The area of expansion must be very carefully chosen.

You now have 10 minutes to transfer your answers to your Answer Sheet.

SPEAKING
(about 16 minutes)

Part 1 Interview (about 3 minutes)

Practise answering these questions:

- Could I just check your name, please?
- Where are you studying? Who do you work for?
- Why did you choose that course / that kind of work?
- Do you think new technology makes our working lives easier or more difficult?
- What hours do most office staff work in your country?
- At what age do you think people should retire from work?

Part 2 Mini-presentation (about 6 minutes)

Choose **one** of three topics, and prepare a short talk on it.

CANDIDATE A

> **A: Personal skills:** the importance of maintaining good relationships with colleagues at all levels

> **B: Management:** how to ensure that time is not wasted during meetings

> **C: Marketing:** how to make an ordinary, inexpensive product seem more attractive

CANDIDATE B

> **A: Travel:** how to make the best use of a long plane journey at the beginning of a business trip

> **B: Personnel management:** how to ensure that part-time staff are treated fairly

> **C: Purchasing:** the importance of considering other factors in addition to cost when purchasing goods or services

Part 3 Collaborative task and discussion (about 7 minutes)

Practise discussing this task and the questions that come after it with your partner.

> **Damage limitation**
>
> Your company has been accused of involvement in a financial scandal, and this has attracted some unwelcome publicity. The Board of Directors has asked you to act immediately to minimize the damage caused by this.
>
> Discuss and decide together:
>
> - what instructions to give to the workforce
> - how to deal with media interest in the situation.
> - how to re-establish public confidence in the company.*

*The third discussion point is used when three candidates take the test together.

Follow-up discussion questions

- What sorts of corrupt or unfair practices can develop in business life?
- What steps can a company take to avoid getting involved in damaging situations?
- What are the characteristics of a healthy company culture?
- How important is PR in helping a company to develop a good public image?

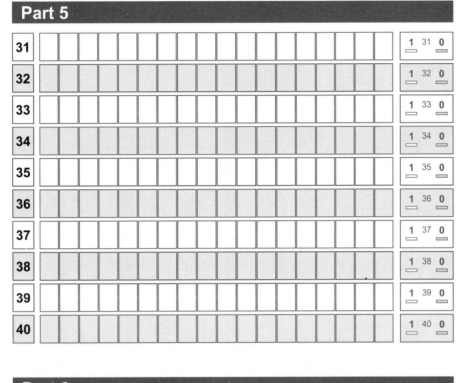

Answer Sheets

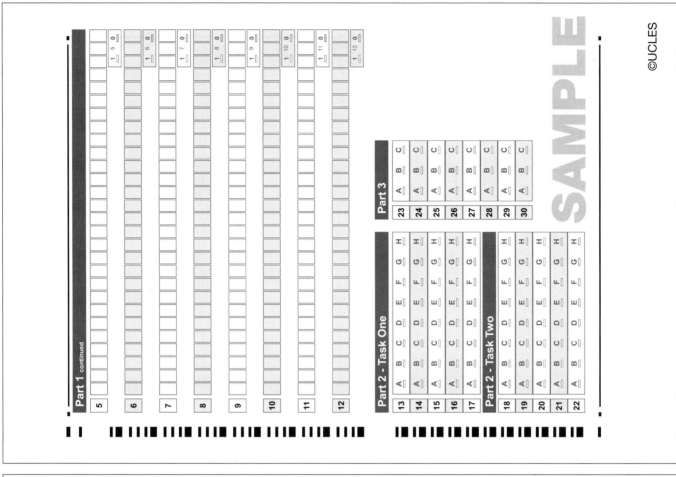
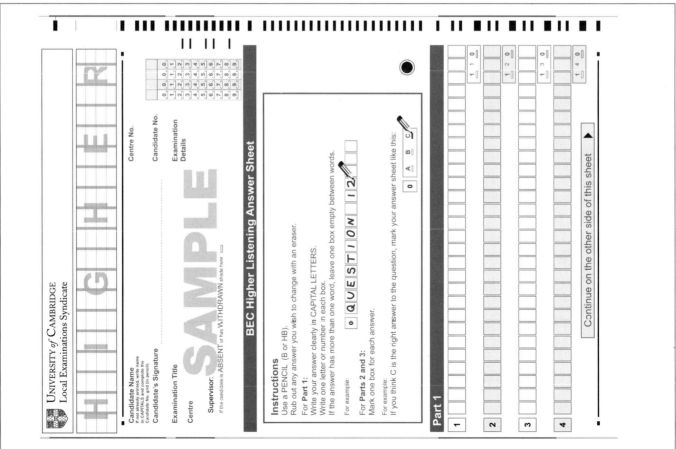

Writing General Mark Scheme

All of these comments should be interpreted at BEC Higher level.

Note: Bands of assessment from 0–5 operate for both Parts, with marks representing how strong or weak the performance is within each band. Marks for Part 2 have a double weighting to reflect the more demanding nature of the task and the greater length of time that candidates will need to spend on it.

Band		Part 1 Mark	Part 2 Mark
5	Full realisation of the task set. • All content points included. • Controlled, natural use of language; minimal errors. • Wide range of structure and vocabulary. • Effectively organised, with appropriate use of cohesive devices. • Register and format consistently appropriate. Very positive effect on the reader.	9 or 10	18 or 20
4	Good realisation of the task set. • All major content points included; possibly minor omissions. • Natural use of language; errors only when complex language is attempted. • Good range of structure and vocabulary. • Generally well-organised, with attention paid to cohesion. • Register and format on the whole appropriate. Positive effect on the reader.	7 or 8	14 or 16
3	Reasonable achievement of the task set. • All major content points included; some minor omissions. • Reasonable control, although a more ambitious attempt at the task may lead to a number of non-impeding errors. • Adequate range of structure and vocabulary. • Organisation and cohesion is satisfactory. • Register and format reasonable, although not entirely successful. Satisfactory effect on the reader.	5 or 6	10 or 12
2	Inadequate attempt at the task set. • Some major content points omitted or inadequately dealt with; possibly some irrelevance. • Errors sometimes obscure communication and are likely to be numerous. • Limited range of structure and vocabulary; language is too elementary for this level. • Content is not clearly organised. • Unsuccessful attempt at appropriate register and format. Negative effect on the reader.	3 or 4	6 or 8
1	Poor attempt at the task set. • Notable content omissions and / or considerable irrelevance. • Serious lack of control; frequent basic errors. • Narrow range of structure and vocabulary. • Lack of organisation. • Little attempt at appropriate register and format. Very negative effect on the reader.	1 or 2	2 or 4
0	Achieves nothing. Either fewer than 25% of the required number of words or totally illegible or totally irrelevant.	0	0

KEY
TEST ONE

READING

Part 1
1. C
2. A
3. D
4. B
5. E
6. E
7. D
8. A

Part 2
9. E
10. A
11. F
12. G
13. B
14. C

Part 3
15. C
16. D
17. A
18. B
19. B
20. D

Part 4
21. C
22. A
23. D
24. D
25. A
26. C
27. B
28. B
29. C
30. A

Part 5
31. by / through
32. did
33. would
34. has
35. to
36. than
37. which
38. that
39. the
40. a

Part 6
41. quite
42. likely
43. too
44. correct
45. correct
46. so
47. being
48. sure
49. kind
50. far
51. While
52. correct

WRITING

General comments on Writing tasks
Writing is assessed on the candidate's ability to fulfil the task, covering all points specified in the question, and using accurate and appropriate language. Writing Part 1 is awarded a mark out of 10, and Part 2 is awarded a mark out of 20.

Part 1

Question 1

Task Specific Mark Scheme
Note: these comments are to be taken in conjunction with the General Mark Scheme on page 81.

Content:
Changes affecting each age group should be mentioned, and there should be some comparison of the age groups with one another.

Organisation:
An introduction and summary are desirable, and details of the changes should be arranged as separate points or paragraphs.

Register:
Register should be consistently neutral or formal.

Range:
Language should cover comparisons, with some linking devices to show contrasts, and vocabulary referring to increase and decrease. Past and present tenses will probably be used.

Target reader:
The target reader should be informed on how the composition of the workforce has changed over twenty years, and know in some detail how each of the five age groups has been affected.

> **Sample Answer**
> *This is a report outlining the changes of workforce of a manufacturing company between the years of 1980 and 2000.*
>
> *The pie chart for 1980 shows more or less an equal part of the age groups. However, in 2000 the pie chart shows a shift of emphasis to employees between 21 to 40.*
>
> *In detail the changes are as follows:*
> *The number of employees between the ages of 16 to 20 years had significantly decreased from 20 to 8 per cent in 2000.*
>
> *On the other hand the age group of 21 to 30 years had a substantial growth from 20 to 45 per cent in 2000.*

> *There was no change of workforce in the age group of 31 to 40 years.*
>
> *The number of employees between the ages of 41 to 50 decreased slightly from 15 to 12 per cent in 2000, in contrast to the employees over 50, who dropped from 15 to 5 per cent in 2000.*

Comments on Sample Answer
This is a good answer which uses all the information displayed in the pie charts. The layout is clear, with a summary of what is shown, followed by points which give further detail. There is some inaccuracy in the use of language ('an equal part of the age groups'), but spelling is accurate and there is a good range of relevant vocabulary (e.g. 'shift of emphasis', 'significantly decreased', substantial growth'). This answer would be likely to receive a mark of about 8.

Part 2

Question 2

Task Specific Mark Scheme
Note: these comments are to be taken in conjunction with the General Mark Scheme on page 81.

Content:
The report must make clear which parts of the contract were successfully fulfilled and which were not, giving details related to the four points specified in the task.

Organisation:
Paragraphing should be used to create a report which is easy to read, and which gives an outline of the situation, some detail on specific points and a clear summary, including a recommendation of future action.

Register:
Clarity and objectivity are essential, as the report would form the basis of an important decision. Register should be consistently formal or neutral.

Range:
There is an opportunity to describe, to evaluate and to make recommendations. Impersonal expressions such as 'it seems' and 'it would appear' would be appropriate, as well as expressions of personal opinion.

Target reader:
The Directors should be fully informed on the situation and the reasons for the concluding recommendation.

> **Sample Answer**
> *This is a report about the IT training service provided to us by firm of consultants CQ Co. over last year. We are not completely satisfy with this service. Although some part of it were good, employes have made some critical feedback. I recommend that we should consider this reaction before we make a decision on whether or not renew the contract.*
>
> *Feedback from employes suggest that the courses at basic level had a good quality and have helped them in their work. Most participants gave favourable feedback, and their managers report beneficial result. On the other hand, we find the more advance course get a more critical response. Many participants in such course report that they are too simple and not specialised enough to the work of our company.*
>
> *Moreover, it seems that the training materials at advance level is full of jargons and trainers' explainations to the questions raised by our staff wasn't clear.*
>
> *We have a very tight budget for staff training, and we find what we have paid is over the budget and the result is not very satisfactory.*
>
> *In summary, I recommend to use CQ only for basic IT course in future and to try to find another way forward for training at advance level.*

Comments on Sample Answer
This is an adequate answer, which covers the required points in a clear series of short paragraphs. There are attempts at linking ('moreover', 'in summary') and a range of relevant vocabulary ('feedback', 'participants', 'budget'). However, there are a number of inaccuracies: 'advance', 'jargons', 'explainations', 'recommend to use' should be 'advanced', 'jargon', 'explanations', 'recommend using' or 'recommend we use'. This answer would be likely to receive a mark of 10 or 12.

Question 3

Task Specific Mark Scheme
Note: these comments are to be taken in conjunction with the General Mark Scheme on page 81.

Content:
The proposal must state clearly the current situation and explain why a change is desirable, covering all three points outlined in the task.

Organisation:
Paragraphing should be used effectively, so that the main points of the proposal can be clearly seen. If brief points are made, complete sentences should still be written.

Register:
A neutral, impersonal register should be used.

Range:
Vocabulary referring to the departments of a company and job titles will be involved. There should be some description, explanation and recommendation of future action. Expressions with 'would', 'should' or 'might' would be appropriate.

Target reader:
The target reader should understand why the change is being proposed and what advantages it would bring.

Sample Answer

To: Head of Human Resources
From: ....
Subject: Introductory video

Background
At present all new employees recruited by our company take part in a one-day introductory programme. They are arranged in small groups and members of the HR department talk to them and answer questions on such topics like the history and structure of the company, pay scales, holiday and pensions, health and safety rules, etc. The proposal is to replace most of this programme with a video.

Advantages of a video
The present system takes up a lot of staff time, especially in the HR department, which is not very cost-effective.
The video could include speeches by key persons such as the Chief Executive and Director of Finance, who don't have time to join in the present programme. They could get known to new staff, and introduce to their own parts of the company.

Parts of the programme to change
Most of the programme can get replaced by the video, except health and safety. We have to keep practical demonstration of fire rules and safety procedures and first aid training.

Staff involved
HR staff would arrange making the video and make the schedule for involving key personnel. An external media consultant will be engaged to direct the video and provide camera crew, etc. and an actor to do voice-over.

Time-scale
It is estimated that the video can be completed by the end of the present year.

Comments on Sample Answer

This is a very good answer, which covers all points fully, with only minimal slips in use of language ('such topics like', 'introduce to' which should be 'such topics as' or 'topics like' and 'introduce' without 'to'). The layout in short paragraphs with titles is helpful to the reader. There is a good range of vocabulary and structures (e.g. passive expressions such as 'will be engaged', 'can be completed'). This answer would be likely to receive a mark of about 18.

Question 4

Task Specific Mark Scheme

Note: these comments are to be taken in conjunction with the General Mark Scheme on page 81.

Content:
The letter must start and finish appropriately. The situation must be made clear and the recipient must be told what to do and what reward to expect.

Organisation:
Clear paragraphing is required.

Register:
The letter is from a company to potential customers who are being persuaded to give some help, so the register should be friendly, while remaining business-like.

Range:
Description of the product, explanation and instructions should all be included. Persuasion and thanks for anticipated co-operation would also be appropriate. Vocabulary will be specific to the product.

Target reader:
The target reader should clearly understand what help the company needs, and what is being offered in return for this.

Sample Answer

Dear Sir or Madam

I am writing to tell you that my company and I have created a new software for your children, helping them with their knowledge. This software is a game. However, they are going to learn a lot with it, and this is free.

Could you, Sir or Madam, try our software on during a month and tell us what you think about it? You will receive our product in one or two days. Would you mind, if this product does not catch your attention, send it back to our company.

To use our software it is really easy. You need only to install it in your computer, following our instructions. After that you can use. You do not need to erase it after the month, since it is yours to keep.

If you decide to try it on during a month, we will send you four questionnaires that you need to send back. This can help us to produce software for you and your children. After this month, you will receive as a present one software of your chose from our catalogue.

We are looking forward to answering all your questions about this new product and we want to create your future.

Yours faithfully

[signature]

Comments on Sample Answer

This is just about an adequate answer, although it is rather short. It conveys all the key points about the situation, and the register is appropriate. However, there is quite a serious lack of control of structure ('try our software *on*' should be 'out', 'one software of your chose' should be 'software of your choice'). 'Would you mind … send it back to our company' should be 'Would you mind sending it back to our company?'. Sometimes this weak structure may obscure meaning ('If this product does not catch your attention' should be 'If this product does not meet your approval' or 'If you are dissatisfied with this product'; 'we want to create your future' is not normal usage and as a result the intended meaning of this phrase is not clear). This answer would be likely to receive a mark of about 10.

LISTENING

Part 1
1. your boss
2. better / bigger offer
3. present his case
4. asked for advice
5. contract
6. trade fairs
7. (personal) appearance
8. senior management/managers
9. £6,000
10. administrative
11. duties
12. job title

Part 2
Task One
13. D
14. G
15. E
16. H
17. A

Task Two
18. H
19. G
20. C
21. F
22. B

Part 3
23. C
24. C
25. A
26. B
27. A
28. B
29. B
30. A

Key Test Two

TEST TWO

READING

Part 1
1 B
2 D
3 E
4 C
5 A
6 C
7 B
8 D

Part 2
9   E
10 G
11 D
12 A
13 F
14 C

Part 3
15 C
16 B
17 C
18 D
19 C
20 A

Part 4
21 C
22 A
23 B
24 D
25 D
26 C
27 A
28 B
29 C
30 D

Part 5
31 their
32 been
33 to / on
34 much
35 However
36 is
37 rather
38 for
39 all
40 as / because / since

Part 6
41 themselves
42 the
43 correct
44 so
45 were
46 a
47 correct
48 for
49 about
50 by
51 including
52 like

WRITING

Part 1
Question 1

Task Specific Mark Scheme
Note: these comments are to be taken in conjunction with the General Mark Scheme on page 81.

Content:
Each stock exchange and each year should be dealt with, and some comparisons made between them.

Organisation:
An introduction and conclusion are desirable, as well as a number of detailed paragraphs or points.

Register:
Register should be neutral.

Range:
Language should relate to rising and falling, and comparisons should be made. Past tense verbs will probably be used.

Target reader:
The target reader should gain some detailed knowledge of what happened to each stock exchange over three years, and how the performance of each compared with that of the others.

> **Sample Answer**
> My observation is that during 1996 Frankfurt has done best, and its trading volume is 30% higher than New York, and three times higher than London. Year 1997 indicates a 20% drop for Frankfurt, which is now nearly the same as New York market. However, this is still 20% higher than London market. Finally, year 1998 bar chart indicates that New York market has soared further and become the largest stock exchange market in the world, while London market has nearly caught up with Frankfurt.
>
> In summary, New York shows a regular increase in the stock exchange dealing, and London showed a similar trend. However the Frankfurt market has dropped to second place, below New York but still ahead of London.

Comments on Sample Answer
This is a good answer, using a range of comparative terms and words related to growth and decline ('drop', 'soared', 'caught up', 'trend'). Linking devices ('however', 'finally', 'in summary') are used. Control of tenses and articles is rather variable, e.g. 'during 1996 Frankfurt has done best' should be '... did best'; 'its trading volume is 30% higher' should be 'was 30% higher'; '... the same as New York market' should be '... the New York market', and 'Finally, year 1998 bar chart' would have been better

phrased as '… the chart for 1998 …'. A probable mark would be about 7.

Part 2

Question 2

Task Specific Mark Scheme
Note: these comments are to be taken in conjunction with the General Mark Scheme on page 81.

Content:
The report must mention concerns over the design of the office and emergency procedures, and also include recommendations.

Organisation:
Paragraphs or numbered or titled points may be used, but however the answer is organised, the concerns must be clearly set out, followed by some recommendations.

Register:
This report is being sent by office workers to a Director of their company on a very serious matter, and should be in a formal or neutral register.

Range:
Vocabulary will be related to health and safety, and the language of description, explanation, suggestion and recommendation will be used.

Target reader:
The target reader should be informed on the dangers present in this workplace, and should understand what changes are being requested.

> **Sample Answer**
> *Since our company is growing rapidly, we can see it lacks adequate provisions for the health and safety of our staff. We have noticed that the design of the office might risk our life. There is no document about the procedures to follow when the emergencies occur. The majority of the staff have no idea about first aid.*
>
> *We think the cables shouldn't be hanging over the floor, because anybody could fall down as they come in the door. Since there are no procedures for dealing with emergencies, if anything happens nobody knows what to do. For example, when a fire is found, they might not know where the extinguishers are, and unable to control the fire. If anybody is injured or stop breathing they may not be able to provide the first aid to the people who need urgent help.*
>
> *Therefore, we strongly suggest you consider the following recommendations.*
>
> *Firstly, please call a designer to change the layout of the office and re-design it with the consideration of safety.*
>
> *Secondly, is it possible to assign an eligible employee to write procedures for dealing with emergencies, issue them to every department and make sure everybody understands?*
>
> *Thirdly, it would be beneficial to both our company and staff if necessary training about the first aid is given to the staff. It may be more effective if some staff could be arranged to attend some fire-fighting performance.*
>
> *We thank you for your kind consideration and action.*

Comments on Sample Answer
This is quite a good answer, which covers all the required points of content. However, although the basic division into description of the problems and suggestions for solutions is made, the problems caused by the design of the office and consideration of emergency procedures are rather confused with each other. The register is also rather too personal, and, in particular, the final sentence and the second recommendation, which is phrased as a question, belong in a letter rather than a report. Use of vocabulary is generally good, but there are a number of minor inaccuracies in language use, e.g. 'might risk our life' should be 'might be dangerous'; 'the emergencies' and 'the first aid' do not require 'the'. This answer would be likely to receive a mark of about 12.

Question 3

Task Specific Mark Scheme
Note: these comments are to be taken in conjunction with the General Mark Scheme on page 81.

Content:
At least three benefits should be mentioned and there should be reference to retaining, reducing and discontinuing at least one, with justifications and some reference to resulting savings.

Organisation:
Some sort of introduction and summary, plus a detailed consideration of each benefit, whether as a paragraph or a numbered or titled point, would be the best way to organise this proposal.

Register:
This is a document for consideration by the Finance Director of a company and should be written in a formal or neutral register.

Range:
Vocabulary will be related to routine aspects of office life, and will include description and suggestions and opinions, together with reasons for these.

Target reader:
The Finance Director should understand which changes to the benefits system are being proposed and the rationale for this. Some indication should also be given of the scope of savings that could be made.

> **Sample Answer**
> *Proposal: Reduction of company welfare benefits.*
>
> *This proposal is based on detailed investigations of the company's welfare benefits.*
>
> *The company offers a number of fringe benefits to the workforce: free coffee, subsidised canteen lunch, free company car and free social events for the employees and their families.*

I suggest the company to reduce the number of the coffees, to retain the subsidised lunches and to discontinue the free social events and the company cars.

The average employee drinks five cups of coffee a day. Each coffee break lasts 15 minutes. As only two breaks are used to socialise with the colleagues, I suggest to reduce the number of free coffees to two. This suggestion brings the company 45 minutes more work per employee and safes the company direct cost of CHF 10,000.

The subsided canteen lunch is a profitable welfare benefit. The employees are more effective in their work when they have eaten a good meal, and the costs are tax deductible.

The participation in free social events for the employees and their families has experienced a significant decline in the last years. The most important reason for this is that traffic has increased by 50%. Most employees prefer to attend social events close to their homes, which they can reach quickly by car or public means of transportation. The offer of social events costs the firm CHF 50.000 a year. This amount can be safed without many regrets.

Lastly, the company offers each manager a free company car. The cars are leased from a car leasing company. The leasing costs mount up to CHF 200.000 a year. I suggest to discontinue this fringe benefit because of its unsocial nature.

Comments on Sample Answer
This is a good answer. The situation is stated and the proposed changes summarized, and then each benefit is considered in detail. All parts of the task are fully covered, with a good range of structure and vocabulary, accurately used apart from a small number of errors ('I suggest … to reduce' should be 'I suggest … reduces' and the less serious error of 'safed' should be 'saved'). This answer would be likely to receive a mark of about 16.

Question 4

Task Specific Mark Scheme
Note: these comments are to be taken in conjunction with the General Mark Scheme on page 81.

Content:
There should be a suitable opening and closing to the fax, an apology and reason for not being available when the visitor arrives, and details of the programme for the stay, including some alternatives, and some other practical details.

Organisation:
The fax should be organised in paragraphs, like a letter.

Register:
The message is for an acquaintance, but in a business context, so it should be friendly, but not too informal.

Range:
There should be a range of expressions relating to the future, and also to the various possibilities available, using, for example, 'could' or 'might'. Vocabulary will be related to workplace activities, travel arrangements, and possibly some tourist or social activity.

Target reader:
The target reader should feel that he or she knows what to expect during the visit, and is informed about all practical arrangements for travel and accommodation.

Sample Answer
Dear…

Your visit

Thank you for your message sent yesterday. As you will be here next week, I think I had better reply quickly.

First of all, I'm very sorry I will not be here to welcome you when you arrive on Tuesday evening. I have to go to Amsterdam for a couple of days. However, I'll be arriving back the same evening, and I'll see you on Wednesday.

Now, about your programme. On Wednesday morning we have made appointments for you with several of the group managers at head office, as you asked. I'll meet you when you arrive, and introduce you them. After lunch, we'd like to take you to visit the new branch office which opened just last month. We've arranged a special dinner for that night, by the way.

On Thursday you will have the opportunity you asked for to talk with John Miller. Various people in Marketing also want to see you while you are here, but I thought you might like to have a free afternoon on Thursday, and go to Marketing on Friday morning before you leave. They will be happy to see you at either time. Let me know what you would prefer to do. If you want to do some sight-seeing on Thursday, I can be available as guide.

When you arrive to the airport, there will be a driver for you. Just look for your name. He'll take you to your hotel, which is the Grand. Next morning, also, a driver will come to bring you to the office at 8.30.

Please contact with my secretary if you have any question. I look forward to seeing you soon.

Yours,

[signature]

Comments on Sample Answer
This is a good answer, covering all the required points and setting them out in clear paragraphs. The use of tenses is well controlled ('I'll be arriving', 'we've arranged') and vocabulary is appropriate. The register is perhaps too informal but still suitable for a business context. There are only minor errors which do not impede understanding ('introduce you them', 'arrive to the airport', 'contact with' should be 'introduce you to them', 'arrive at', and 'contact' without 'with'). This answer would be likely to receive a mark of about 16.

LISTENING

Part 1
1. (draft) minutes
2. queries / questions / problems
3. project plan
4. action points
5. postponed / re-arranged
6. 07712 351816
7. security badge
8. internal
9. IT L/liaison G/group
10. agenda
11. Q/quarterly R/report
12. end of April

Part 2
Task One
13. C
14. B
15. A
16. G
17. F

Task Two
18. D
19. H
20. F
21. G
22. E

Part 3
23. C
24. A
25. B
26. A
27. B
28. C
29. A
30. C

TEST THREE

READING

Part 1
1. C
2. D
3. B
4. C
5. E
6. E
7. A
8. A

Part 2
9. A
10. G
11. D
12. F
13. E
14. B

Part 3
15. A
16. D
17. B
18. C
19. A
20. D

Part 4
21. D
22. A
23. B
24. B
25. C
26. A
27. C
28. B
29. D
30. D

Part 5
31. To
32. At
33. takes
34. there
35. such
36. the
37. too
38. long
39. what
40. each / every

Part 6
41. period
42. how
43. if
44. correct
45. but
46. with
47. correct
48. and
49. these
50. above
51. correct
52. that

WRITING

Part 1

Question 1

Task Specific Mark Scheme
Note: these comments are to be taken in conjunction with the General Mark Scheme on page 81.

Content:
The sales pattern of each of the three magazines should be mentioned, and comparisons made between them.

Organisation:
There should be some introduction of the topic, and a summary of findings as well as a detailed comparison of the performance of the three magazines over five years.

Register:
Register should be neutral.

Range:
Language should refer to growth and decline as well as to comparisons between the magazines. Past tense verbs will probably be used.

Target reader:
The reader should be fully informed on the relative performance of the three magazines over a five-year period.

> **Sample Answer**
> This is a report comparing the performance of the three teenage magazines, Magic, Sparks and Wavy, from 1995 until 2000.
>
> It can be seen that Sparks magazine started in best position in 1995, and its sales increased until 1997. Since then, sales are decreasing sharply. It has become least selling magazine.
>
> On the other hand, Magic started with lowest position, but the sales increased sharply for one year, then became more stable, and continue slow increase.
>
> In 1995 Wavy was in worse position than Sparks, and sales fell for the next two years. But then they rose dramatically, and in 2000 it was in first place.
>
> To sum up: Magic shows stable growth over five years, Wavy has very rapid growth in last three years and Sparks has dramatic decline.

Comments on Sample Answer
This is quite a good answer, which both summarises the information given and goes into some detail for each magazine. Presentation is clear, with introductory and concluding paragraphs. There is a good variety of relevant vocabulary ('decreasing sharply', 'rose dramatically, 'stable growth'). Language errors (missing articles, prepositions, e.g. 'with lowest position' should be 'in the lowest position', 'very rapid growth in last three years' should be 'a very rapid growth in the last three

years') do not impede understanding. This answer would be likely to receive a mark of about 7.

Part 2

Question 2

Task Specific Mark Scheme
Note: these comments are to be taken in conjunction with the General Mark Scheme on page 81.

Content:
The report must include some general comments about the event, as well as covering the four specified points.

Organisation:
It must be organised either in paragraphs or in a series of points. If numbered points are used, it is still necessary to write complete sentences.

Register:
Personal opinions can be given, but the register of the report needs to be formal or neutral.

Range:
This should be a past tense account, but can also include expressions of opinion and recommendations for the future.

Target reader:
The manager should get a clear picture of the importance of the event, and be able to judge whether future participation is likely to be worthwhile.

> **Sample Answer**
> *This report is about the recent trade fair held two weeks ago in China. It was a major event for a medium company like us to attend first time in a foreign country.*
> *Last week, thousands of computer hardware manufacturers congregated in the international trade fair in Beijing, China. Many famous giant companies, such as Microsoft, IBM, Compaq had a considerable exhibition on the new style of laptops and desktop computers.*
> *We are small brand to be known by the overseas customers. However, we tried our best to attract attention from all participants. We had bright, colourful advertisement signs over all our stand. We paid a little more to get an outstanding location, which was right opposite the main entrance.*
> *We had attracted many wholesalers and retailers from Asian countries, which is our goal to trade with them. Many companies indicated that they wish to trade with us if there are no language barriers. Fortunately we found people from Singapore, Taiwan, Hong Kong and China could speak fluent English.*
> *Asia has huge markets, especially China, which is the market most European companies intend to enter and penetrate. We have kept many of the Chinese companies who have the interest to trade with us. It is a golden opportunity to expand our markets globally. Therefore, any chance of trade fairs like this in future,*
> *we should not miss, and should even take more extensive display space.*

Comments on Sample Answer
This is an adequate answer, which covers all the specified points and attempts to develop them fully. The two introductory paragraphs could be more clearly organised, but there is a clear concluding paragraph. The range of vocabulary used relates well to the topic ('outstanding location', 'wholesalers and retailers', 'expand our markets'), but use of structure is not always under control (e.g. 'We are small brand to be known' should be 'We are too small to be known overseas' and 'who have the interest to trade with us' should be 'who are interested in trading with us'). This can affect the reader's understanding, although this is not a general problem. This answer would be likely to receive a mark of 10 or 12.

Question 3

Task Specific Mark Scheme
Note: these comments are to be taken in conjunction with the General Mark Scheme on page 81.

Content:
The problem must be stated and all four of the suggested solutions described.

Organisation:
An introductory paragraph followed by separate paragraphs for each of the suggested solutions is the most obvious way to structure the answer.

Register:
Register should be neutral. The proposal is for colleagues, but should not be very informal.

Range:
Vocabulary will be related to office life. The language of description, suggestion and speculation will probably be used. There may be use of conditional structures.

Target reader:
The group manager and other colleagues should have a clear idea of the changes they are being asked to consider.

> **Sample Answer**
> **The Problem**
> *As we have a lot of people in this office working at small individual work-stations, with compueters and phones, it is difficult to concentrate because of people talking and making phone calls. All previous attempts to reduce noise levels have failed. This is a serious problem, as we suspect that it is affect our productivity.*
> **Solutions proposed**
> *No more space can be made available, but it is proposed that we consider the following possibilities.*
> **1. Introducing rules on socialising in the office**
> *This would mean that all coffee breaks have to be taken in the canteen, and it is not allowed to eat or drink at a work station. This would cut down noise and also*

keeps the office cleaner!
2. Flexible office hours
If we could all choose to come to work as early as seven a.m., and leave as late as nine p.m., there would be fewer people in the office together, so it would be quieter. However, it would be more difficult to arrange meetings and work together with colleagues at all.
3. Changes in office layout
A corner of the office could be created as a 'quiet area' by partitions. However, this would make all the work-stations even smaller than now. Another idea is to put higher partitions between small groups of two or three people.
4. Working at home
It is suggested that most of us have certain parts of our jobs (e.g. writing reports) that could be done at home. This could mean coming to the office only on two or three days every week. This would make it easier to do work you have to concentrate on in a quiet place. This would have to be a voluntary arrangement, just for people who choose it, and the company would have to supply compueters, modems, etc.

Please be prepared to give feedback on all these ideas at a meeting to be arranged in the last week of March.

Comments on Sample Answer
This is a very good answer, which covers all points in the question and is clearly organised, with an introduction, numbered paragraphs and a final sentence telling the reader what to do next. Most of the language is concerned with possibilities (with 'would' and 'could') but there is also some descriptive language and an instruction. There are only minimal errors ('compueter', 'is affect', 'keeps' should be 'computer', 'is affecting' and 'keep'). This answer would be likely to receive a mark of 18 or 20.

Question 4

Task Specific Mark Scheme
Note: these comments are to be taken in conjunction with the General Mark Scheme on page 81.

Content:
The letter needs to have an appropriate beginning and end, and cover all four points listed in the task.

Organisation:
It should have an appropriate beginning and end, and be organised in paragraphs.

Register:
The letter is to a potential employee of the company, so the register should be neutral or formal.

Range:
Language of description, instructions and explanation will be required, and vocabulary related to selection procedures and travel arrangements.

Target reader:
The short-listed applicants should know what to expect during the visit, as well as practical arrangements for how to get to the company.

Sample Answer
Dear Applicant

You have been selected as a potential future employee of our company by the recruiting committee.

Therefore, we would like to invite you to our internal assessment day at which you will have tests and interviews and get further information about SIMUL Ltd.

We kindly ask you to prepare the following documents and bring them with you:

   Please write at least one page on your future objectives, personal and profession (hand writing)

   Please select one of the enclosed drawings and be prepared to describe what you see on it and what feelings you have while looking at it.

The assessment takes place on 15 May from 9.00 to 18.00, and will only be interupted by a two-hour lunch break. While the morning is reserved for several tests and interviews, the afternoon offers you the chance to get a first impression of our company. You will be visiting different working places of SIMUL Ltd., such as the factory, the marketing offices and our large store.

Please refer to the enclosed situation plan if you intend to come by car. There is plenty of parking space. If you choose the train, please take line 17, leaving the main station at 8.15 on track 5. Get off the train at Acorn Road, walk down Lime Street, and turn left after 600 feet, where you will see our premises. The reception is in building A.

We are looking forward to welcoming you on 15 May to our assessment day. If you have any questions, please do not hesitate to contact us under 01 1235 17 28.

Yours faithfully

[signature]

Comments on Sample Answer
This is a good answer, which covers all necessary elements of the task, is well organised and achieves a register which is welcoming as well as businesslike. The final paragraph is appropriate, but such a letter would probably finish with 'Yours sincerely'. Vocabulary is appropriate and the range of language varied, with correct use of tenses, polite commands and conditionals. There are a few small errors ('interupted', 'under' + phone number should be 'interrupted' and 'on' + phone number), which do not impede comprehension. This answer would be likely to receive a mark of about 16.

LISTENING

Part 1
1. mobile phone
2. handouts
3. feedback form
4. e-mail addresses
5. networking
6. airport minibus
7. 10.30
8. exhibition stands
9. workshop session
10. main hall
11. government support
12. riverboat trip

Part 2
Task One
13. D
14. F
15. B
16. A
17. H

Task Two
18. E
19. F
20. A
21. G
22. C

Part 3
23. A
24. C
25. A
26. B
27. A
28. A
29. B
30. C

TEST FOUR

READING

Part 1
1. C
2. A
3. B
4. E
5. D
6. B
7. C
8. E

Part 2
9. G
10. A
11. B
12. F
13. D
14. C

Part 3
15. A
16. D
17. B
18. C
19. D
20. B

Part 4
21. B
22. C
23. D
24. C
25. C
26. A
27. A
28. D
29. C
30. B

Part 5
31. where
32. as
33. who
34. the
35. of
36. did
37. up
38. being / getting
39. much
40. another

Part 6
41. in
42. was
43. with
44. therefore
45. out
46. correct
47. else
48. correct
49. should
50. as
51. to
52. even

WRITING

Part 1

Question 1

Task Specific Mark Scheme
Note: these comments are to be taken in conjunction with the General Mark Scheme on page 81.

Content:
The weekly pattern of sales for both men's and women's clothes should be mentioned, and they should be compared.

Organisation:
There should be an introduction and a summary of the pattern which emerges, as well as some paragraphs or points dealing with detail.

Register:
Register should be neutral.

Range:
There should be a range of expressions related to the rise and fall of sales and to comparisons between sales of men's clothes and those of women's clothes. Verbs will probably be present tense.

Target reader:
The reader should be informed about the differences and similarities between sales of men's clothes and sales of women's clothes.

Sample Answer
As clearly highlighted by the chart, the general tendency or message is that men usually do their shopping during the weekend, while women spread their shopping more over the days of the week.

Sales of both men's and women's clothes made by the Fitz shops are very low on Monday and Tuesday. While sales of women's clothes rise suddenly to 10% of the total for the week on Wednesday and Friday, they decrease on Thursday. Sales of men's clothes remain generally slow until Friday.

Sales of clothes for men and women rise sharply to their highest level during the weekend. Sales of men's clothes are particularly high on Saturday but decrease slightly on Sunday. On the other hand, sales of women's clothes increase steadily from Friday to Sunday, when they reach their highest level.

Comments on Sample Answer
This is a good answer, giving both a summary of what is shown, and a detailed comparison of sales of men's and women's clothes. It is clearly arranged as three paragraphs, and generally very accurate in the use of structure and vocabulary. There is a range of suitable expressions ('decrease slightly', 'reach their highest level') and a limited attempt to use linking devices to point

up comparisons ('while', 'on the other hand'). This answer would be likely to receive a mark of 8.

Part 2

Question 2

Task Specific Mark Scheme
Note: these comments are to be taken in conjunction with the General Mark Scheme on page 81.

Content:
The report should cover all aspects of the specific problem described in the task, and also include general recommendations.

Organisation:
The problem must be stated at the beginning of the report, various points must be dealt with and there must be some kind of conclusion and recommendations. These can be laid out as a series of paragraphs or as headed points.

Register:
As this is a serious matter, the register should be neutral or formal.

Range:
Vocabulary will relate to the behaviour of staff, and there will be description of past events, expression of opinions, and suggestions and recommendations.

Target reader:
The target reader should understand why complaints have been made, and the extent of the problem, and should know what is going to be done to tackle it.

Sample Answer
This report summarises the investigations made regarding the complaints of external callers and visitors about the attitude of some of our employees.

Problem
External callers and visitors have seriously complained about the following inappropriate and unprofessional treatment:

The response to their questions, enquiries and even orders was very slow. It sometimes lasted up to one week until they got a first reaction.

The treatment both on the phone as well as visiting our offices was more than frosty. Callers and visitors used the word 'unpolite'. They felt unwelcome and said that they got the impression to bother or disturb our employees.

Recommended Measures
It is questioned whether disciplinary action is appropriate in the first instance. But the employees concerned should certainly be warned and disciplinary action should be announced in case of one further complaint.

The situation has to be monitored very closely. Specific and professional training on customer focus, service-minded behaviour and the art of communication is highly recommended. Corresponding proposals and offers from trainers have already been collected.

Clear targets for customer care must be set as follows:
Every caller and visitor is treated as a customer.

Every request, enquiry, question, etc. is responded to within one day, at least giving a preliminary information and a time frame for when the final answer can be expected.

Every visitor is received as our guest: politely and courtesly.

All of our employees must be aware that the contacts, via the phone or personal, are our 'business card' towards external partners.

Conclusion
The problem is severe and measures must be taken quickly. We risk to jeopardize the reputation of the company.

Comments on Sample Answer
This is quite a good answer. All points are covered thoroughly, and layout is clear. The register is appropriate, and there is a good range of vocabulary. However, there are some mistakes ('unpolite', 'they got the impression to bother', 'courtesly', 'we risk to jeopardize' should be 'impolite', 'they had the impression they were bothering …', 'courteously', and 'we risk jeopardizing'). This answer would be likely to receive a mark of about 14.

Question 3

Task Specific Mark Scheme
Note: these comments are to be taken in conjunction with the General Mark Scheme on page 81.

Content:
The duties involved in the present post should be outlined, as well as the changes proposed.

Organisation:
Either paragraphs or headed or numbered points should be used.

Register:
The register should be neutral, as the communication is between colleagues, but in a business context.

Range:
Language of description and explanation referring to the present should be used, and there will also be reference to the future, with possible use of conditionals. Vocabulary will refer to tasks related to office work.

Target reader:
The reader should gain a clear idea of the writer's present job, how it can be developed, and the changes and benefits this would create.

> **Sample Answer**
> This proposal refers to the post of general assistant in the Marketing Department (which I hold at present) and suggests ways in which it could be developed.
>
> The post, which I have done for three years, is general office duties, such as filing, writing letters and faxes, and typing materials for several managers. Quite often power-point presentations and seminar materials have to be prepared either for managers or for external consultants who they commission to run marketing presentations. What I notice is sometimes two people prepare quite similar materials, but they don't use each other's. Also, they both might be trying to commission the same consultant, and they don't always know who is good and who is not so useful.
>
> What I propose is this: a centralized system of presentations, and a database to keep records of consultants, so that all knowledge of these things is shared. I would like to set up the database and keep the presentation materials updated as part of my job.
>
> In order to develop the skills to do these things, I would need only some short advanced courses, as I have some knowledge of databases from my initial training at college, and I have learned about power-point by using it and studying the manual. I have researched local firms which provide short courses, and some will come to your office to do that, so that not so much time is needed away from your job.
>
> I do not think I would need to give up any of my present duties, because they are declining in any case. More managers now do his own correspondence by e-mail, and there is less need for filing or sending faxes. In busy times perhaps we could get a temporary clerk to do those things.
>
> Finally, I think this would benefit the company because we would get a more efficient system for seminars and presentations, and we could better control our using external consultants, which could maybe save some money.

Comments on Sample Answer
This is quite a good answer, covering all required points. There is a good range of vocabulary and use of structure ('set up the database', 'keep the presentation materials updated'). However, the style is a little rambling and informal, with some errors ('do his own correspondence', 'we could better control our using' should be 'their own correspondence', and 'we could control our use of external consultants better'). The final paragraph is a little vague, and doesn't explain how money would be saved. This answer would be likely to receive a mark of about 14.

Question 4

Task Specific Mark Scheme
Note: these comments are to be taken in conjunction with the General Mark Scheme on page 81.

Content:
This should include some information on both the company's product and the rival product, and it should be clear why the rival product poses a threat. (The term 'product' should be taken to include services.)

Organisation:
There should be some division into points or paragraphs.

Register:
E-mails are normally written in a fairly informal style, but this one is to a senior colleague, so should be informal to neutral.

Range:
Language should be mainly descriptive, reporting information. There may be suggestions and speculation. There should be some vocabulary related to the type of product under discussion.

Target reader:
The target reader should understand the situation and why it might cause concern.

> **Sample Answer**
> Simon – I heard something the other day which I think you should know about – though possibly you already do. Just by chance I ran into someone I know who writes on consumer affairs, and she told me that one of our rivals (she wouldn't say who) is developing the technology to put some new security systems on the market which will be way ahead of anything we have at present.
>
> Apparently these devices will be suitable for houses and cars. They might be quite expensive when they first appear, but prices could come down quite rapidly. The advantage is that they are very easy to install and use, and much less easy for thiefes to disable than anything you can buy now. And apparently there's far less risk of them going off by accident and annoying the neighbours.
>
> My contact doesn't know how long it will be before these devices appear on the market. But I imagine this could be a big threat to our Car Protector system. At present market reports all put it well ahead of rival products on value for money and reliability. It's been a steady seller, and we weren't considering replacing it for a year or two yet. Should we be worried?
>
> Can you see if Phil knows anything about this? I can try to find out more if you want me to. I'll be in the office tomorrow if you want to talk.

Comments on Sample Answer
This is a very good answer, dealing with all the required points, although the last point is covered minimally. The language is quite clear and correct, although informal, with just a couple of errors in spelling ('affaires', 'thiefes' should be 'affairs' and 'thieves'). This answer would be likely to receive a mark of 18 or 20.

LISTENING

Part 1
1. (major) airports
2. launch
3. 500
4. business environment
5. photocopying / photocopy / photocopies
6. (flexible) layout
7. flipcharts
8. free accommodation
9. modem points
10. health club
11. venue(-)finding
12. no-quibble

Part 2
Task One
13. G
14. C
15. H
16. E
17. A

Task Two
18. C
19. B
20. G
21. F
22. A

Part 3
23. B
24. A
25. C
26. A
27. B
28. C
29. A
30. C

TAPESCRIPTS

TEST ONE

PART 1

Questions 1 – 12

You will hear part of a radio programme in which someone is talking about how to get a pay rise. As you listen, for questions 1 to 12, complete the notes using up to three words or a number.

You will hear the recording twice. You have forty-five seconds to read through the notes.

Now listen and complete the notes.

F: …the next topic in today's programme is the interesting problem of how to get a pay rise, and I've been talking to a few people with recent experience of this situation. You know you deserve to be paid more – but how do you convince your boss of that? Here are some of their ideas. See what *you* think about them.

Let's start with Mark, who is a television producer – in a way he represents the ideal way to get a pay rise – have a better offer from someone else up your sleeve. Mark was being offered a large amount, more than his current salary, to go to another company, so he was able to go to his manager and see if he could negotiate an even bigger offer to stay. But, as Mark points out, the trick here is not to look greedy or disloyal – he made a big effort to present his case in the right way. He says you should never try to bully your way to a better salary. He approached it not as demanding something but as asking for advice, and that got him the result he wanted.

Now, you may not be as fortunate as Mark, so what can you do if you haven't got another job lined up? Simon, who works in human resource management, thinks you could do what he did, and try 'overdelivery' – that means doing a lot more than just what is stated in your contract. So, for example, he volunteered to look after visitors to his firm, and he gave up free time at weekends to go to trade fairs and conferences. But he says always remember you have to make sure the right people know you're doing all this, because your aim is to impress them, not just to take on a lot of extra work!

Talking of which, how about this idea from Claire, who works in PR. See what you think. Claire felt she was very competent, she was doing good work, but she wasn't getting much credit for it, so she decided she would spend a lot of money on her personal appearance. She had an expensive new haircut, bought some eye-catching designer clothes, took a lot more trouble with her make-up – and she told me it worked! She says senior management suddenly started to appreciate the quality of her work, although it didn't actually change in any way. It was just that they started to notice her existence, and in due course she managed to get a rise of £6,000! I have to confess, I feel a bit sceptical about this story – but why not give it a try and let me know if it works for you.

To finish with, let's just take a look at what happened to Sarah. She had a pretty ordinary sort of post as an administrative assistant, but she used her initiative to develop it into something much more demanding, and then she wanted some reward for that. She went to her manager, with a list showing all the duties she had started with, and what she had added to the job. She was asking for a £2,000 rise and a new job title. Now, I think that was a perfectly reasonable thing to do, but her manager just turned her down flat and said, 'What you've done is all fine and good, but we want you to do the job we appointed you to do'. So, Sarah failed to get a rise, but she then began to look around for a new job, and she eventually found one with a much higher salary. So there you are – if you know you're worth it, one way or another, you can't lose!

Now you will hear the recording again.

That is the end of Part One. You now have twenty seconds to check your answers.

PART 2

Questions 13 – 22

You will hear five people talking on the phone about a problem which has occurred at work. For each extract there are two tasks. Look at Task One. For each question 13 to 17, choose the type of problem which has occurred from the list A to H. Now look at Task Two. For each question 18 to 22, choose the action each person is taking from the list A to H.

You will hear the recording twice. You have thirty seconds to read the two lists.

Now listen and do the two tasks.

M1: OK, now as I understand it, you were told it was being sent out about ten days ago, around the seventeenth, so it does begin to look a bit as if it's gone astray. And, let me just check a few things with you, you've asked around at your end, so you're sure it's not just sitting in goods-in, or reception or somewhere. OK. And it's a pretty big, bulky box-full, not some little thing that could easily get overlooked. Right. So, the first thing I'll do, I'll send an e-mail around everyone in the department here, asking them to have a good look for it, just in case it never left us. Then if it doesn't turn up in the next day or so, we'll think again. What? Hang on! We're a long way from talking about compensation at this stage!

F1: No, there's no mistake on our part at all. He assured me it would be with us by the end of the month, and this assurance was not fulfilled. Absolutely. Yes, of course I've got it in writing – yes, no problem putting my hands on the evidence of the actual delivery date. It's a clear failure on their part to keep their side of the bargain, there's no question at all about it. OK, I know it's serious, yes, I know all about the knock-on effect on our schedules, but I think we've got to begin by giving them a chance to explain themselves, if they can. So I'm going to start by copying all the relevant documentation to them, which clearly states the agreed schedules, confronting them with the evidence, and then we'll see what they have to say for themselves.

M2: It isn't as if it's the first time this has happened, either. No, well, this time it looks as if it might have happened in transit, because the packaging is all ripped open, and then of course it didn't protect the contents, and the consequence is they're not in a fit state to use. Well, it isn't a case of asking for financial recompense, I don't think, at this stage, because we've got this history of incidents like this. I'm beginning to be more of the opinion that we should be considering a change of supplier, but to be fair to them, I think we should write to them first and let them know that we're not happy, let them know that we're thinking of making a change unless they can guarantee an immediate improvement.

F2: I'm not blaming anyone for this, not yet, but I do want to find out how it happened so we can take steps to ensure it doesn't happen again. It's too late now to do anything except damage limitation this time round. They've come back from the printers, we've even started mailing them to clients, and *then* someone goes and notices! Makes us all look a right bunch of idiots. Anyway, thinking of the future, we'll need to have a look at our procedures, maybe build in some extra external checking. So this is what I'd like from you, by the end of this week, a brief summary of the present system, and your suggestions on the way forward. Just a page or two, with a couple of action points, should be enough.

M3: Right, I see, so you ordered the white one and what we sent you was the same model, but in cream. Well, I must apologise, first of all, because it does look as if we've made a mistake. The thing is, I'm very sorry, but the reason we were offering the reduced price was because they were the last few left, the end of a discontinued line, so I'm afraid we can't now replace the one you've got with the other colour, because I know we haven't got any left. All we can do is tear up your cheque, so you get your goods totally free of cost, and, as I say, we hope you'll accept our sincere apologies for this.

Now you will hear the recording again.

That is the end of Part Two.

PART 3

Questions 23 – 30

You will hear part of a radio interview with a successful young businessman called Jonathan Elvidge. For each question 23 to 30, mark one letter A, B or C for the correct answer.

You will hear the recording twice. You have forty-five seconds to read through the questions.

Now listen and mark A, B or C.

[I = Interviewer; J = Jonathan Elvidge]

I: ...and today our guest is Jonathan Elvidge, managing director of the Gadget Shop, a rapidly expanding chain of retail outlets which all started here in the city of Hull in the north of England. Hello, Jonathan.

J: Hello.

I: Now the first thing I want to ask you about is what made you want to open a shop. Is your family in retail, or had you studied business at all?

J: No, nothing like that. I did go to college, but I dropped out of the course after a year and got a job with a local insurance firm. Mind you, I always fancied the idea of being my own boss one day.

I: So where did the Gadget Shop idea come from?

J: Well, like a lot of men, I'm not much good at shopping, especially choosing the right presents for other people, and what I always needed myself was one shop where I could go – say before Christmas – and just buy lots of presents in one go. I talked to friends about it, and they all liked the idea, too.

I: So, one-stop shopping – that's the Gadget Shop concept.

J: Yeah. That's it.

I: So, how did you go about turning your idea into a reality?

J: Well, I thought about it for years, and my friends kept encouraging me to have a go, but I didn't want to rush into anything. What I did do was read an awful lot of books – books were like my business advisers. I studied the lives of people who had become successful entrepreneurs and learnt from their experiences.

I: Were you well prepared, do you think, to start a business?

J: I thought I was, but in fact it very nearly all went wrong at the very start.

I: What happened?

J: Well, I found a shop I wanted to rent – it was in a new shopping mall just being built. I raised some money by re-mortgaging my flat and the bank agreed to loan me the rest. But they made the loan conditional on my opening the shop by a certain date, and then the building work got behind schedule, the date passed, and the bank withdrew their offer.

I: You must have felt pretty desperate at that point.

J: Yeah, you could say that... No job, no shop... Anyway, luckily enough, I remembered reading about a government scheme to loan money to new small businesses, so I rushed off an application. It was accepted, and as soon as the builders were out, I was in there, getting my shop set up.

I: And what were the early days like? Was it hard to build up business?

J: Surprisingly easy, really – right from the start I could see I'd been right. The shop was always packed with people, the stuff just walked off the shelves.

I: So you got rich – end of story?

J: Not so, I'm afraid! I was only just breaking even. Trouble was, I was on a prime city-centre site, and the rent was sky high. Being a mere beginner in retail, I'd made a beginner's mistake. I didn't realise all the other shops had negotiated their rents with the mall, while I'd just said 'yes' straight away to what they asked me, which was far too much.

I: A very frustrating situation. How did you manage to break out of it?

J: I had to do something I'd never planned on doing – take on a partner. In fact what happened was, somebody called Andrew Hobbs approached me. He was already established in business locally, and he saw the potential of the Gadget Shop, and thought I should be expanding my operation by opening up on some new sites in other northern cities. I liked his suggestions, so he injected some capital, I gave up fifty per cent of the business, and that was it. It all took off.

I: And I believe you've now got over thirty shops?

J: Yeah – we opened two in London last year, and we've now got our first overseas branch – in Amsterdam. Our next venture's going to be into TV selling – we're investing quite a lot of money in a new shopping network. Risky business, but could be very big for us, if it all works out. It's a challenge all right, but I like that – I get a real buzz from it.

I: Right! So tell me, how about on-line shopping – have you considered that?

Now you will hear the recording again.

That is the end of Part Three. You now have ten minutes to transfer your answers to your Answer Sheet.

TEST TWO

PART 1

Questions 1 – 12

You will hear a recorded message left by a senior manager for his personal assistant. As you listen, for questions 1 to 12, complete the notes using up to three words or a number.

You will hear the recording twice. You have forty-five seconds to read through the notes.

Now listen and complete the notes.

M: Hi, Jo. This is Peter. It's 4.15, Sunday. I've got a bit of an unexpected family crisis on, which means that in about 20 minutes I have to leave to get on a flight to Dublin, so this seems the best way to ask you to hold the fort in my absence. I'll ring in some time on Monday, OK? Sorry to do this to you, but I'm sure you'll cope!

Right, now the first thing is the minutes from last week's Senior Management Group Meeting. I've e-mailed you my amendments to the draft, so could you please see that those are made, and then get them sent out? If you have any queries, consult Sophie, but it should all be clear, I think. Oh, don't forget, we circulated copies of a project plan before the meeting. The updated version of that needs to be attached to the minutes as an appendix. Oh, and will you please issue a firm reminder to everyone who attends these meetings to look for any action points with their name on them, and to get on and see to them promptly? Otherwise, they can sometimes get forgotten.

OK, now Monday's appointments. I've already managed to speak to Liz Newton about the meeting I was going to have with her at 10. We've agreed to postpone it – er, remind me to tell you the new arrangement when I get back – I can't remember all the details just now, but that has been taken care of. However, I *will* need you to call up Malcolm Vinall and explain to him that I'm not available for our meeting at 2.15. Call him on his mobile – the number is 07712 351816 – that's your best bet for getting to him in time. Apologise profusely on my behalf – I've already had to put him off once. Actually, now I come to think of it – ask him if Friday is any use to him. Suggest he comes in about 11.30 and I'll take him out for lunch. If he can make it, you'll need to book him a parking space and have a security badge ready for him in reception when he comes in. The rest of Monday I'm just scheduled to see internal people – can you look in the diary and then let them know I've had to go off? See if you can re-schedule them for some time next week.

Right, that's the most urgent things taken care of. Here are a few other things I'd like you to get on with if you find you have time. We've got an IT Liaison Group coming up, so could you do the usual for that – make sure we have a room booked, arrange coffee, send a reminder round to everyone who attends, and make a start on the agenda?

One last thing. Could you ring Reprographics and ask if they've done those copies of the Quarterly Report I asked for yet? They hadn't reached me when I looked in on Saturday morning, although I'm pretty sure I asked to have them by the end of April. If they don't turn up very soon I shall want to know what's going on.

That's it, I think. Must get going. I'll try to have a word with you tomorrow and with any luck, I'll be back in the office on Wednesday. Bye!

Now you will hear the recording again.

That is the end of Part One. You now have twenty seconds to check your answers.

PART 2

Questions 13 – 22

You will hear five people talking about the restructuring of the company they work for. For each extract there are two tasks. Look at Task One. For each question 13 to 17 choose the type of job each person does from the list A to H. Now look at Task Two. For each question 18 to 22 choose the reaction each person has to the changes being made to the company from the list A to H.

You will hear the recording twice. You have thirty seconds to read the two lists.

Now listen and do the two tasks.

F1: In the area I work in, what we've been experiencing over the last few years is expansion rather than job losses, so I personally don't feel any threat from the restructuring. I haven't been with the company for all that long, so I don't remember the old days, but I gather that there was a time when people expected goods to sell themselves – the attitude was, if you have a quality product, there's no need to get out there and shout about it. Well, we know better now! I think this division will do well out of the restructuring. Personally, I don't expect to enjoy the process – I imagine we have a stressful time coming – but actually I'm pretty confident that my own post will be upgraded. I'll be very disappointed if it isn't!

Tapescripts   Test Two

M1: We've been hearing rumours about this restructuring for a long time, not that anyone has bothered to discuss it with us properly, and I don't really know yet what effect it will have on me and my job. What I think is, automation of the plant has already gone as far as it can go. The workforce in the factories themselves was cut to the bone years ago from what it used to be when I started here, and I don't see how they can make any more reductions in the area I work in – so I don't honestly know what it's all about. As far as I can see, everything works fine as it is, so why not leave us alone to get on with it?

F2: I've been here for more years than I care to remember, started as a junior when it was still quite a small place, before the new building was opened. Of course there were no computers then, no fax machines, or even photocopiers when I started! It's strange to think of now, how much things have changed in this job. No one works for just one boss any more, the way we used to, and a lot of the managers do their own typing and filing now. I reckon it's all less interesting than it used to be, and with these new changes coming in, I've started to feel I've been here long enough. I'm old enough to get offered a good financial package if I go early, so that's what I've decided to do. I'm finishing at the end of this month.

M2: If the number of employees the company has goes down, which is very likely, then our division will be one of the places where cuts get made, which won't be very good news for me. I don't want to leave, having just bought a flat here. It wouldn't be easy to get an equivalent job in the same part of town. Mind you, I've built up some useful experience in the short time I've been here – been involved in work on the new performance assessment scheme we've just brought in for all employees, as well as a fair amount of advertising for and interviewing temps. Only trouble is, because I haven't been working here long, mine could be one of the first posts to be cut.

F3: This whole idea of restructuring is in fact something which I've been hoping to see come about for some time, so I'm extremely pleased now that we've been told it's all definitely going ahead. I think really it's impossible for an old established firm like this one to adapt to present-day business conditions without undergoing some radical changes. Of course, in a way, I'm actually part of the process of change – only a few years ago, jobs like mine didn't even exist! It's got to happen, and in fact I'll actually be developing some of the software to make it possible. So of course I'm *very* much in favour of this restructuring!

Now you will hear the recording again.

That is the end of Part Two.

PART 3

Questions 23 – 30

You will hear part of a radio discussion on an issue concerning health at work. An expert called Sarah Baylis is being interviewed. For each question 23 to 30, mark one letter A, B or C for the correct answer.

You will hear the recording twice. You have forty-five seconds to read through the questions.

Now listen and mark A, B or C.

[I = Interviewer; S = Sarah Baylis]

I: Our topic today is one which affects us all – the health of the workforce. Downsizing has left companies with smaller numbers of employees, so staff absences affect results even more than they used to. Here to comment on how to avoid losing money this way I'd like to welcome Sarah Baylis, author of *The Healthy Company*. Hello, Sarah.

S: Hello.

I: Now, poor health in the workforce costs money, doesn't it?

S: Yes it does, and in several ways. There are direct costs – benefits paid during absence, costs of early retirement – and also lots of indirect costs – employing replacement workers, training costs, revenue lost while new staff settle in. And there may be lowered staff morale and loss of customer confidence, too.

I: Is it the same picture in all kinds of companies?

S: No, there are differences. The highest levels of absence are in the public sector – the health service, for example – where the work is notoriously stressful. High-tech companies, in contrast to this, have a good record – low rates of absence – perhaps because they have a younger workforce – and the retail trade also tends to keep very tight control of absences, possibly because of its emphasis on client-facing activities.

I: I see! So how much does sickness actually cost companies? Do you have any figures for us?

S: Yes, I do. It's been calculated that a typical UK firm loses eight days per person per year in short-term absences. The direct costs are about £700 – that's benefits paid to the sick employee. Then there are the indirect costs of employing a replacement and the loss in efficiency that causes, and that's estimated at £1,200, making a total of almost £2,000 per employee.

I: And that's just short-term absence.

S: Yes. We have to add to that the cost of long-term absence. Now, here's another aspect of the problem. In the past, companies used to early-retire sick employees, but now pension funds are not as fat as

102

I: they used to be, so for many firms that's becoming too expensive to be an attractive option. Plus, you have new legislation like the Disability Discrimination Act, which can make it much harder to early-retire staff.

I: Mmm. So what makes people too ill to work? Is there a pattern?

S: Oh, certainly, and, interestingly, it's a changing pattern. In the past, long-term absence was linked to heart disease and cancers – now it's more often caused by mental conditions, including stress, and musculo-skeletal problems. And the causes of short-term absence have changed, too. A lot of that is linked to stress, alcohol, smoking, things like that.

I: So, what can a company do?

S: Well, it's essential to control the cost of all this. You have to intervene, and you have to target that intervention wisely, to reduce absence in the most cost-effective way you can. Actually, you need to consider an employee's health over their whole working life, not just when they're sick, so you can avoid problems before they even arise.

I: Can you give us an example of how this works?

S: OK. Here's an example from a London hospital. They were getting a lot of sickness absence and high staff turnover, caused by manual handling injuries. Lifting patients and moving heavy goods was leading to a lot of back injuries. So, they brought in a system of manual handling support which involved training, bringing in some new equipment and the introduction of policies and procedures for lifting and other manual handling. Result? A massive decrease in absences.

I: Sarah, time is running out, sadly! Could you just sum up for us your advice on managing the problem of absence?

S: OK, well, the secret is to develop the right procedures for managing the problem, and to use financial mechanisms to reduce the impact on the business. Some effective measures I would go for are early retirement where appropriate, wise use of benefits, ongoing monitoring of short-term absence – and using insurance to protect your company's results.

I: And that's all we have time for. Thank you.

Now you will hear the recording again.

That is the end of Part Three. You have ten minutes to transfer your answers to your Answer Sheet.

Tapescripts   Test Three

TEST THREE

PART 1

Questions 1 – 12

You will hear the organiser of an international conference welcoming delegates to the final day, and giving details of the programme. As you listen, for questions 1 to 12, complete the notes using up to three words or a number.

You will hear the recording twice. You have forty-five seconds to read through the notes.

Now listen and complete the notes.

M: Good morning, hello. Right. Welcome, everybody, to the final full day of this conference on the development of small and medium enterprises, SMEs, as we call them, in eastern Europe. Just before we start, we've just got a few announcements and reminders to go through. Yes, come on in, there's plenty of room down at the front here!

OK, now, I've got a bit of lost property here. Does anyone recognise this camera? Good, right, pass it back, would you? And this mobile phone? Dr Steadman? OK, there we are.

Let's see now. Yes, could you pass these round please? It's the handouts from yesterday afternoon's session, which some people were asking for. Do take one if you didn't get one yesterday. And while we're at it, could I also please ask everyone here to take one of these feedback forms, fill it in and leave it in the box at reception? It's very helpful for us when we're planning future events of this kind if you can do that.

We'd also like to be able to ensure the continuation of some of the very useful contacts made here between people from various countries and organisations, so I'm going to pass around this list and ask you to add your contact details, especially your e-mail addresses, if you wouldn't mind. Of course, if you don't want your address on this list, that's fine, feel free to just ignore it – but I would say that this conference has provided us all with an excellent opportunity for networking, and that's something we'd like to encourage.

Now, some of you, I know, are having to start leaving this afternoon to catch planes home this evening, so could I ask those people to be ready with their baggage in reception at about 10 to 5. At 5 o'clock sharp the airport minibus will be arriving, and the driver is only allowed to park here for a few minutes to pick you up, so please be on time. And, while we're on the topic of leaving arrangements, if you are staying another night, can I remind you that tomorrow morning breakfast will be served from 7.30 to 9.15, and then you must check out of your rooms by 10.30 at the latest. And now, the final reminder of this kind – to all of you who have been responsible for exhibition stands – we do need you to get them taken down and packed up this evening. Please don't be tempted to leave it till tomorrow morning to do that.

Right, well, before we think about leaving we still have a full day ahead of us, so let's get on. However, there are just a few things to note about the arrangements for today. The venue for the 11.30 workshop session, to be led by Anne Kramer, has changed. It will *not* now take place in seminar room B, as stated on your programme, but we've moved it to the main hall. That's to give you all a bit more space. And Dr Jakubowski has asked me to correct the title of his presentation, which takes place at 2 o'clock this afternoon. That should read, 'Applying for Government Support for SMEs: a brief guide'.

Finally, for those who will still be here this evening, something has been arranged for you, and that is a riverboat trip, with, so I'm told, a very interesting commentary, which is available in more than twenty languages, on the history of the city. If you intend to go on that trip, could you speak to Judith before lunch time today, and let her know…

Now you will hear the recording again.

That is the end of Part One. You now have twenty seconds to check your answers.

PART 2

Questions 13 – 22

You will hear five people talking about the services their small firms provide to a large company. For each extract there are two tasks. Look at Task One. For each question 13 to 17 choose the type of service each firm provides from the list A to H. Now look at Task Two. For each question 18 to 22 choose the special advantage of the service each firm offers, from the list A to H.

You will hear the recording twice. You have thirty seconds to read the two lists.

Now listen and do the two tasks.

F1: Well, we get quite a lot of business from them, especially at particular times of the year, either when they're especially busy or summer holidays, winter, times like that when people might be off sick more. They'll ring up desperate suddenly, people off with flu or something, nobody to do the typing or answer the phones. We usually have no difficulty finding someone with the right sort of qualifications and experience to fill the gap. We try to get someone along the same day – that's our stated aim, to get a suitable person into the post before a crisis develops. We react to demand quickly – I think that's what gives us the edge on other agencies, and what got us this contract.

M1: We were very pleased to get the contract with this company, because, of course, they're very big, and so there's a lot of movement of personnel, especially among the younger, junior people, and that tends to create a need for our services. They call us in, oh, every couple of months, usually for a group of six to ten people, for anything from a half day to a couple of days, usually for something IT-related – advanced computer skills, spreadsheets, using graphics, that sort of thing. *We* go to *them* – they've got all the equipment, what we supply is people with the latest knowledge and skills. We pride ourselves on employing the cream – people who are bang up to date with developments, have lots of relevant experience, and are able to communicate it all successfully to others.

F2: They've signed us up to look after their premises in general, interior and exterior – that means we do outside windows and the car park and surrounding grounds as well as the offices themselves. And indoors it includes carpets, all the washrooms and the kitchen and the staff canteen. So, it's a big contract for us, and we want to hang on to it. In our line, a lot of the employees are more or less unskilled, quite a few are part-timers, so it's not always, let's say, an easy workforce to manage. But we put all our efforts into making sure they do a really good, thorough job – no cutting corners, no rush jobs. Every last little thing is done properly. That's what puts us ahead of the competition.

M2: Of course, a company the size they are generates a fair amount of business for people like us, and we do the lot for them. See, we can offer them local and long distance, seven days a week, twenty-four hours a day, same day as well as next-day deliveries. We've got a variety of vehicles – bikes and vans. Now, a lot of other people could offer that, but we've got more – for instance, we're fully insured for fragile goods, and we're even licensed to carry dangerous goods, if that should ever arise. We can handle anything – documents and small packages up to pallets. Whatever's needed, we can do it. That's why we're the best!

F3: We get quite a lot of business from them, well, it goes up and down, really, according to how busy they are. It's when they've taken on a lot of temporary staff they tend to call us because then they know they're going to be setting up extra work stations, so they'll need more computers, etcetera, but it's only on a short-term basis, so they're not going to want to invest money in purchasing a lot of new hardware. We come along and install it all for them for a fixed term, and then take it away when the need for it has gone. We can put in good quality equipment at a very competitive rate, so that's why, in my opinion, they come to us every time.

Now you will hear the recording again.

That is the end of Part Two.

PART 3

Questions 23 – 30

You will hear part of a job interview. A Human Resources officer, James, and a manager, Anna, are interviewing Karen for the post of P.A. to Anna. For each question 23 to 30, mark one letter A, B or C, for the correct answer.

You will hear the recording twice. You have forty-five seconds to read through the questions.

Now listen and mark A, B or C.

[J = James; A = Anna; K = Karen]

J: OK, Karen, to start with, would you just run us through your CV? Tell us what you've done.

K: Right. After I left school I took a year off so that I could earn some money and then go travelling for a bit before I went to college. I did some office jobs at that time, and I also worked as a guide – taking groups of foreign visitors round. I did that partly to prepare for studying European languages at college. After college I was planning to teach, but then I got a summer job in an office, and it worked out so well, I just stayed there.

J: So, tell us a bit more about that job.

K: Well, it was with quite a small firm, and my boss, Mr Howard, was often out of the office. I used to take all his phone messages and open his mail. Then I'd go through his diary and set up appointments for him, if necessary. Generally, I'd say I organised his office life for him.

J: It sounds as if he gave you a lot of trust and opportunities to develop the job.

K: Yes, he did. I was extremely lucky. We just always got on well together, and worked as a team.

A: So what made you leave, Karen? You stayed quite a long time, didn't you?

K: More than five years, yes. Well, I enjoyed it, and I probably would have stayed longer, but Mr Howard actually took early retirement, and after he went there was a general restructuring, a lot of things and people changed, and I decided to have a change too.

A: OK, now this job, as you know, consists mainly of P.A. duties for me. Can you tell us what in particular made you apply for it?

K: Yes. When I saw the advert, I thought, well, a lot of it sounds similar to what I've been doing, and at the same sort of level. But in a bigger firm I'd have a chance to learn some new things. I'd like to make some progress now, add some new skills to what I can already do.

A: And the money's better.

K: Well, yes, that always helps!

A: OK, well, let me tell you a little more about what the job involves, assuming we were to offer it to you. Like your old boss, I'm out a lot, in fact I do quite a lot of trips abroad, so you'd have to keep things going for me while I'm away. Your languages might come in handy, as we have a lot of overseas clients, but I've got to say that a lot of the work is pretty routine and unglamorous. You won't get to travel yourself, or have much contact with the clients.

K: No, I realise that.

A: What you will do is a certain amount of correspondence, although the more basic office work – photocopying, filing, sending faxes – you can pass on to a junior or a temp. You won't need to do that. You'll also prepare powerpoint presentations for me, which will give you a chance to develop some new computer skills. What else? Well, I tend to type up my own reports, but you'll prepare agendas for the meetings I have here, and be there with me to take the minutes.

K: That all sounds fine. It's what I expected.

A: Good. James?

J: One more question, Karen. It can get quite pressured in this office sometimes, everyone in a rush, a lot of noise, and you have to be in the midst of that and deal with it and keep going. Tell us what particular qualities you think you've got that would help you do that.

K: Goodness! Well, of course I have had at times to make decisions for myself and cope with some unexpected situations, so… I'd say the thing about me is, I can't bear letting other people down. If I say I'll do something it means I will, even if there's a lot going on, so I have to stay late to get it done.

J: Thank you, Karen. That's all we want to ask you. Now, is there anything you'd like to ask or check with us?

K: Well, I've read all the information about the grade of the post on the salary scale and about leave entitlement, so I understand all that. Oh, one thing. I believe you operate some sort of flexi-time system. Would it be up to me to decide when to come in?

J: OK, I'll just briefly explain our system to you. What we have here is a limited form of flexible working, which just allows you to…

Now you will hear the recording again.

That is the end of Part Three. You now have ten minutes to transfer your answers to your Answer Sheet.

TEST FOUR

PART 1

Questions 1 – 12

You will hear part of a presentation about the business services offered by a chain of hotels. As you listen, for questions 1 to 12, complete the notes using up to three words or a number.

You will hear the recording twice. You have forty-five seconds to read through the notes.

Now listen and complete the notes.

F1: Welcome, everybody, and thanks for coming along. We've brought you all together today because you are all people who organise a lot of meetings and other kinds of events, large and small, and we want to introduce you to all the services which we can now offer you, to make your lives easier! Now we'll have time to chat later over a buffet lunch, but first I'd like to show you this brief video, and then I'll answer any initial questions you may have. OK?

F2: The *Elite* service. A complete service for all business meetings. *Elite* is a network of over 60 modern hotels, all of which are situated in easily accessible locations, in or near key cities or at major airports. We understand how important it is for us to meet the particular needs of your business, and so we've designed our business packages to be flexible. We can cater for anything from a small meeting to a multi-location conference, an exhibition or a product launch. We can give you a small seminar room for fewer than six people for a meeting lasting hours, or a suite of rooms, accommodating up to 500 visitors, for several days.

Many of our hotels now include self-contained conference and training suites. These suites provide a business environment which is purpose-built, closed off from the hotel's tourist and leisure facilities, with state-of-the-art meeting rooms and dedicated reception areas in which a full range of office services, such as fax and photocopying, are available. In order to accommodate a wide range of event types, flexible layout is a feature of all rooms designed for small- to medium-sized meetings, with adjustable lighting and leading edge AV equipment, including working walls, PA systems and multi-computer connection facilities. Equipment such as overhead projectors and flipcharts is standard in all meeting rooms.

We are able to offer conference delegates an eight-hour package, comprising room and equipment hire and table refreshments, or a twenty-four-hour package, which also includes a three-course dinner, overnight accommodation, breakfast, and free accommodation for delegates' partners.

We at *Elite* recognise that at the end of the day, conference delegates may wish to relax or to continue working, so all bedrooms are fitted with desks and modem points, as well as interactive TV with a range of sports and entertainment channels. All rooms have en suite bath and shower. The majority of our hotels now have their own health club, with swimming pool, fully equipped gym and dance studio, which can be used by conference delegates at no extra cost. Every one of our hotels offers a choice of several bars and restaurants, where a variety of international and traditional dishes can be enjoyed.

When you need to arrange a meeting, large or small, remember, we provide a free venue-finding service. We have professional meeting and conference organisers at every venue, to help *you* organise your event from start to finish. The same organiser will ensure that you receive written confirmation of all your requirements within 24 hours of your making the booking, and will remain your point of contact throughout your event. Booking is easy with our all-inclusive products and straightforward pricing, and our no-quibble bill policy means that if anything goes wrong and we can't fix it, we don't charge you for it.

Let *Elite* work with you – together, we're a success.

F1: OK. Now, I'm ready to answer any questions you may have.

Now you will hear the recording again.

That is the end of Part One. You now have twenty seconds to check your answers.

PART 2

Questions 13 – 22

You will hear five people talking about courses they have been on at work. For each extract there are two tasks. Look at Task One. For each question 13 to 17 choose the title of the course each person has been on from the list A to H. Now look at Task Two. For each question 18 to 22 choose the criticism of the course that each person expresses from the list A to H.

You will hear the recording twice. You have thirty seconds to read the two lists.

Now listen and do the two tasks.

M1: I went along with high hopes, because it was something I was really interested in finding out about. I'd decided I had to get up-to-date with something that's going to change all our lives so much. Well, he was a good teacher, very friendly and enthusiastic, and he didn't assume any prior knowledge, which was right for me! The trouble was, he talked a lot about how we could use it to access information, and he gave us plenty of advice on how to use it effectively, but what we didn't get was enough real hands-on experience. So, now I feel I know all about it, but I'm less confident that I actually can use it properly. I still need someone to sit at my machine with me and take me through some examples.

F1: This was a useful course, because it's an area I do sometimes get involved in, and of course it's a very sensitive area, where you need to develop techniques for dealing with people who are often in an angry or aggressive state. You have to learn to be calm and defuse a situation before it gets out of control, and at the same time you have to be able to make a rapid assessment of what's going on. She based the sessions on small group work on a series of cases, so we had some realistic material to work on, which was excellent, but the problem was there were so many new ideas to take in, so much to think about packed into each session. It was stimulating but I felt it was all too pressured, and I ended up feeling exhausted.

M2: I fully accept that this is a very important aspect of life in any large organisation like ours, where you don't automatically see people on a day-to-day basis, and you need to make sure the right people get the right information – whether it's going up or down the chain of command or across departments. However, I would question whether sending us on this type of course is the best use of resources we can come up with. I don't actually feel that we have a problem with this aspect of business life. We're an organisation where, on the whole, people *do* interact well with one another, and we all have all kinds of means of passing on information – e-mail, voice-mail and so on. Why we wasted time and money on this course, I really don't know!

F2: This is a course I was very keen to get a place on, because it's something I feel a lack of in my own educational background, something I haven't ever studied in the formal sense. Having said that, I've obviously had to pick up whatever's relevant to my own job, and I've never been afraid of numbers, when I know the context they're being used in. So, when I was presented with something aimed at complete beginners, I can't say I found it much of a challenge. I felt he knew his stuff, but he'd just pitched it too low for the majority of us, and we didn't learn a great deal that we didn't know already.

M3: It was a brief down-to-earth session, which it was important we all attended. And I think we all found it quite interesting and enlightening to do so. We needed to find out exactly what the new government legislation demands of us. It can be tedious when new directives of this type are introduced, but I think we must all recognise that it's in our interests to keep the threat of work-related accidents or sickness – and hence absenteeism – to a minimum. Pity he couldn't have made it a bit more interesting, though. He wasn't an outstandingly clear or lively speaker, and his overheads and the handouts he gave us were, quite frankly, scruffy, badly produced, not at all professional – which I found rather surprising.

Now you will hear the recording again.

That is the end of Part Two.

PART 3

Questions 23 – 30

You will hear part of a radio programme called 'Ask an Expert'. A management consultant called Leo McBride is being interviewed. For each question 23 to 30, mark one letter A, B or C for the correct answer.

You will hear the recording twice. You have forty-five seconds to read through the questions.

Now listen and mark A, B or C.

[I = Interviewer; L = Leo]

I: And next in today's 'Ask an Expert' I'd like to welcome management consultant and expert on mergers, Leo McBride. Leo, hello.

L: Hello.

I: Leo, there've been a lot of mergers in the news recently, so the question I'd like you to address for us is this: Is it possible for a company ever to get too big? What's your feeling on that?

L: Well, as you might expect me to say, it all depends. It certainly *isn't* true any more that physical size *alone* – by which I mean a large asset base, big workforce, high sales and so on – is good. On the other hand, being big, in the traditional sense of having plenty of assets, *is* still important. As long as those assets are developed and managed properly, then you can't have too much. But size is just part of the picture, not the whole picture. What really matters most, in my opinion, is market capitalisation.

I: Which is?

L: Quite simply, market capitalisation measures the value placed on a company by the market. You need a big market capitalisation in order to take advantage of the opportunities for growth which we're now getting from globalisation. The fastest way to grow is by acquiring other companies, so there's a lot of buying going on. If you have a big market capitalisation, then it's easy and cheap for you to expand by buying other companies, and it's relatively hard for other companies to buy you.

I: So, what produces a big market capitalisation?

L: Two things – physical size and performance. By performance I mean, of course, the returns you get on your capital. So you see, you could have two companies – one bigger in terms of capital but getting only modest returns on that capital; the other one smaller in size but performing better. In terms of market capitalisation, they could both be at the same level.

I: So, what does this mean in the global economy we live in now?

L: OK, now if you're a small company, and not performing well, you're in trouble. Being big can be an advantage, but being small and performing well is also good. The point to understand is this: a company with big assets could still risk being taken over by a smaller company which has better performance. This does actually happen – I could give you several recent examples.

I: So, what does a company need to build up a position of power in today's global capital markets?

L: There are two important factors – intangible capital and specialisation. Let me explain.

I: Please do!

L: Firstly, intangible capital. Now, in our global capital markets it's quite easy for any decent company to raise capital. You don't need to be big to do that. What you've got to have is something to make you more attractive to investment than your competitors – and that is this so-called intangible capital – things like skills, expertise, knowledge, and so on.

I: Right.

L: Secondly, the digital revolution in technology means that you can now base your business on much narrower specialisation than before. Why? Well, accessing customers over a wider area of the world is becoming easier, so you can have a very narrow focus and still develop a big customer base. Another thing. It's getting cheaper all the time to interact with other companies. Result: you can stick to just doing the things you're really good at and outsource everything else to other people. In the past you couldn't do that – it cost less to do it *all* inside the company.

I: Uh-huh. So, can it be a good idea for a company to have more than one area of specialisation?

L: Oh yes, it's often a good idea. To add a further area of specialisation can be very beneficial. But a note of caution here – if you find yourself getting into some kind of activity where your intangible capital is weak, you're doing it wrong. A company's size must be firmly based on the intangible capital it has. That's a golden rule for growth.

I: Leo, I'm afraid we have to stop there. Many thanks for all the insights you've offered us.

L: It's been a pleasure.

Now you will hear the recording again.

That is the end of Part Three. You now have ten minutes to transfer your answers to your Answer Sheet.

Speaking Assessment Criteria

Assessment
Candidates are assessed on their own performance and not in relation to each other according to the following analytical criteria; Grammar and Vocabulary, Discourse Management, Pronunciation and Interactive Communication. These criteria are interpreted at Higher level. Assessment is based on performance in the whole test and is not related to particular parts of the test.

Both examiners assess the candidates. The Assessor applies detailed, analytical scales, and the Interlocutor applies a Global Achievement Scale which is based on the analytical scales.

Grammar and Vocabulary
This refers to range and accuracy as well as the appropriate use of grammatical and lexical forms. At BEC Higher level a range of grammar and vocabulary is needed to deal with the tasks.
At this level grammar is mainly accurate and vocabulary is used effectively.

Discourse Management
This refers to the coherence, extent and relevance of each candidate's individual performance. Contributions should be adequate to deal with the BEC Higher level tasks. Candidates should produce utterances which are appropriate in length.

Pronunciation
This refers to the candidates' ability to produce comprehensible utterances. At BEC Higher level, meanings are conveyed through the appropriate use of stress, rhythm, intonation and clear individual sounds, although there may be occasional difficulty for the listener.

Interactive Communication
This refers to the candidate's ability to take an active part in the development of the discourse. At BEC Higher level, candidates should be sensitive to turn-taking throughout most of the test and hesitation should not demand patience of the listener.